Invisible victims

Invisible victims

crime and abuse against people with learning disabilities

Christopher Williams

Jessica Kingsley Publishers
London and Bristol, Pennsylvania

The Joseph Rowntree Foundation has supported this project as part of its programme of research and innovative development projects, which it hopes will be of value to policy makers and practitioners. The facts presented and views expressed in this report, however, are those of the authors and not necessarily those of the Foundation.

First published in the United Kingdom in 1995 by
Jessica Kingsley Publishers Ltd
116 Pentonville Road
London N1 9JB, England
and
1900 Frost Road, Suite 101
Bristol, PA 19007, U S A

Library of Congress Cataloging in Publication Data
A CIP catalogue record for this book is available from the Library of Congress

British Library Cataloguing in Publication Data
A CIP catalogue record for this book is available from the British Library

ISBN 1-85302-309-4

Printed and Bound in Great Britain by
Cromwell Press, Melksham, Wiltshire

Contents

Contents

Elaborated Contents

Acknowledgements

Thanks to

Louise Bashford
Tarnjit Birdi
Hilary Brown
Ray Bull
Elaine Crick
Kate Eldon
Margaret Flynn
Michelle McCarthy
Suk-Tak Tam
Satinath Sarangi
Lydia Sinclair
Peter Stephens
Linda Ward
members of London People First
colleagues at the Norah Fry Research Centre

for thoughtful and supportive comments on drafts of this book and related publications. (Final responsibility for the content does, of course, rest with the author.)

Louise Bashford
Karen Gyde
Lorna Henry
Ruth Foster

for excellent administrative support.

Karen Gyde

for outstanding design and production work.

Sheena MacKenzie

for dissemination and production support.

Introduction

Mary was assaulted. Her handbag was stolen and she received hospital treatment for a bone fracture. The police caught a group of youths with Mary's handbag as they were assaulting someone else. But the youths were not charged in connection with Mary, and she heard no more.

John was assaulted. He stated that he received injuries amounting to a patch of reddening on his chest and an ankle graze for which no treatment was necessary. There was no corroborating evidence that the injuries resulted from the assault. His assailant was charged, found guilty and fined, and ordered to pay compensation for the injuries.

Mary has learning disabilities; John does not. Why is it so difficult to achieve justice in an equitable manner for victims with learning disabilities? What can be done to improve the situation? These are the key questions that this book addresses.

The first part of *Invisible Victims* outlines the range and nature of victimization against people with learning disabilities reported as part of a two-year research project supported by the Joseph Rowntree Foundation. The victimization is put in the context of relevant legislation, because many taken-for-granted happenings in the lives of people with learning disabilities are more than 'abuse' or 'harassment' – they are clearly crimes. One of the principal lessons is that our awareness of victims with learning disabilities is usually in relation to a single event, yet all too often they have a history of cumulative victimization at schools, in institutions, and in the community that is unique and usually overlooked.

Chapter Two discusses the sources of victimization, and highlights the point that the main perpetrator groups do not fit our normal perceptions of 'offenders'. This increases their potential power over their victims, and helps to explain why so much victimization is unrecognized.

The starting point for achieving equitable justice for people with learning disabilities is to increase the visibility of the problem and of the perpetrators. Chapters One and Two provide the background for achieving this generally, or more formally through staff training.

Chapter Three deals with prevention, emphasizing that the primary resource for developing preventive strategies is people with learning disabilities themselves. The proposals are of most relevance to those working regularly with potential victims, but also provide some fresh insights for professionals in the general field of crime prevention.

Chapter Four discusses the question of reporting, and emphasizes that there is a trend towards more direct reporting to the police. Future debate should not be concerned with whether or not to report, but with how the police should then respond. The greatest reporting block is the linear, 'chain' reporting networks which currently exist in service settings – one broken link and the report fails to get through. It is proposed that 'reporting webs' are a better way to conceptualize what is needed. At present the debate about reporting is mainly in the domain of service policy-makers who inevitably have vested, institutional interests, often of control and management rather than facilitation. The reporting debate should instead become led by actual and potential victims and their supporters.

The latter part of the book outlines how to achieve redress for victims with learning disabilities through the police and the courts, and creative alternatives to these usual channels. This is essentially a 'handbook' for action for those supporting victims. But the discussion is also addressed to those who control and maintain the 'invisible' barriers which at present inhibit the achievement of justice for people with learning disabilities. Proposals include simple reforms derived from instances of good practice in the UK and abroad.

Finally, why are people with learning disabilities 'invisible victims'? Drawing together strands from the research provides answers which will relate to other minority groups in similar circumstances.

Criminal victimization is the main focus of the book, together with civil law where relevant, but other forms of victimization are also important. Inappropriate police behaviour, abuse within the justice system, insensitive media reporting, and 'disablist abuse' (which equates with racial abuse), are examples of victimization reported by people with learning disabilities as having a very negative effect on their lives.

Whilst 'abuse' is not usually covered by national legislation, European Law is clearly relevant, and abuses of power do fall within the ambit of the UN *Declaration on Victims of Crime and of Abuse of Power* (1985). The Declaration covers 'Persons who...have suffered harm, including acts or omissions that do not yet constitute violations of national criminal laws but of internationally recognized norms relating to human rights' The Declaration suggests that states should develop legislation and provide 'remedies to victims...[including] restitution and/ or compensation, and necessary...social assistance and support.' Some countries (eg Australia, Canada, Barbados) have managed to enact legislation dealing with sexual harassment, which clearly reflects the ethos of the UN Declaration (see CSDHA 1992: 13). This demonstrates the possibilities of developing legislation in relation to 'abuse' which may be on the margins of the law.

The distinction between 'crime' and 'abuse' is important. Frequently, the language used concerning people with learning disabilities diminishes the seriousness of an incident. Inappropriate terms are transferred from the field of child victimization (where they are often equally incorrect). For a person with learning disabilities we use 'sexual abuse', when for another woman we would say 'rape' or 'sexual assault'; 'abuse' of someone with learning disabilities is often an 'assault' of anyone else; most 'financial abuse' is really theft.

Invisible Victims is intended as a basis for action. It includes material and ideas for staff training, and clear policy proposals. Contact addresses, for further information, are given throughout, and the discussion is illustrated with victims' stories, press reports, and relevant law extracts. The main policy considerations are repeated at the end of the book. These provide the means to open a discussion about crime against people with learning disabilities to a variety of audiences – victims, perpetrators, carers, professionals in care services and the justice system, and the general public.

Note
1. *Invisible Victims* is not a law book, although every effort has been made to ensure accuracy.

2. Much of the data in *Invisible Victims* comes directly from victims. In many circumstances ethical considerations preclude the level of validation of information that would be usual. (For example, if a woman reports that she was tied up by step-parents in her youth, there is little that can safely be done to check this without questioning the victim's truthfulness in a way that might be harmful.) Therefore examples should be taken as illustrating arguments and recommendations. Much identifying detail has been changed, except where victims have expressed the view that they would like to be known.

3. The term 'learning disabilities' has been used to identify a group of people otherwise described by terms such as 'mentally handicapped', 'intellectually disabled', 'people with learning difficulties', and, in North America, 'mentally retarded'. Whilst it is a convenient generalization, the label 'learning disabilities' is arbitrary and always questionable concerning people who are, as a result of formal assessments, borderline cases. The adoption of a group approach to this aspect of victimology should not be taken as an argument for special laws or special treatment, but, rather, for anti-discriminatory practice to permit equitable justice irrespective of the labels people have.

1

CHAPTER

What is happening?

What type of victimization is suffered by people with learning disabilities and how does the law relate to this? The questions are important because surveys such as the *British Crime Survey* rarely, if ever, include people with learning disabilities. Group homes and similar places, where people under Health or Social Services care live, are excluded from government surveys because they are considered 'institutions'.

Even if people with learning disabilities are included in surveys, they are not identified as a distinct group. No attention can be given to their, often unique, circumstances. This is in contrast to other minority groups who may be vulnerable, for example, because of race, gender or age.

According to Home Office statistics, resulting from surveys, about one third of recorded crimes in the UK concerns cars, and 94% property in general. From these figures alone it is obvious that the nature of crime against people with learning disabilities will be very different – they rarely own cars and usually have relatively little property. Based on statistics which largely exclude people with learning disabilities, current crime prevention, detection and redress policies will relate to a perceived majority need.

It is helpful to view examples of victimization in the context of the laws to which they should relate. The results may come as a surprise to professionals who are involved with people with learning disabilities, and carers. A knowledge of how the law should work in favour of victims with learning disabilities is a key element in helping them achieve justice.

Unlawful killings

One of the most disturbing aspects of collecting information about crime against people with learning disabilities is the number of reports of unlawful killings that, even without making a systematic effort to search, come to light.

A classic case of murder, which clearly seems related to the vulnerability of the victim, happened in Bristol in 1992. Brian Newman, who was aged 54, left his regular pub at 11 o'clock, having missed the last bus, intending to walk the mile to his home. On his way home he was brutally attacked and murdered, for the purpose, it seems, of stealing about £10. The murderer, a young man who was psychotic, was finally caught because he attacked another man of 18, causing him brain damage.

As always in such cases, the victim is not just one person. Brian Newman's father told a local paper simply, 'That's my life gone.' Members of the day centre attended by Brian Newman were also affected by his death. One woman, whilst shopping in a supermarket many months later, became bothered and said, 'Perhaps he's in here – the man who did the murder.'

Sometimes the circumstances of death do not have the usual victim–victimizer relationship. One of the saddest situations concerned a mother and father who committed suicide, by attaching a pipe from the exhaust of their car to the interior, also killing their 22-year-old daughter who had learning disabilities. The family had constantly complained about the services they received, and suicide had been mentioned in relation to this disappointment. An instance which entailed a direct failure of care concerned a young man who choked to death eating a sandwich, although his eating disabilities were well known. Other deaths within care settings, where there is not a clear perpetrator–victim relationship are considered later in terms of *Organizational Victimization* (see Chapter 2).

The actions of perpetrators are sometimes incomprehensible. In 1992 the *Guardian* reported a case at Reading Crown Court in which a 44-year-old cleaner, who was

> 'backward and illiterate died after his 'guardian' forced him to stand in an icy lake on the end of a rope... David Miller was repeatedly hauled to the bank to be given a beating.' (16 September 1992: 3)

Death may result from more indirect causes. *The Times* reported the case of a man with learning disabilities who jumped to his death from a shopping centre after youths taunted him and shouted, 'We want to see some blood.' A police spokesman commented,

> 'With a bit of gentle persuasion he would probably have come down... It was disgusting behaviour to provoke this poor man. They were ghoulish yobs.' (9 January 1984: 2)

A number of deaths are also caused, deliberately or otherwise, by other people with learning disabilities. Arson seems a particular danger.

Detectives believe a fire at a nursing home, which killed three residents, may have been started deliberately. Police began forensic checks after reports of an altercation between two residents... police said a 'murder style' inquiry had been set-up... A fourth victim of the fire...is in intensive care suffering from burns and smoke inhalation.

The Guardian, 20 May 1992: 3

There are minor incidents with major repercussions, such as the man who died following a 'scuffle' with another resident which triggered a rare heart condition. Peer victimization is discussed more fully later, but the crucial point is that it is not restricted to petty offences.

Stories of unlawful killings might support arguments that people should not be moved into community settings. It is as well, therefore, to remember that people did, and still do, die from unnatural causes within long-stay hospitals.

Living in the community can be dangerous for people with learning disabilities, as for anyone. But in addition, care settings which are supposed to be safe seem potentially life-threatening to an inexcusable degree.

Abduction

In 1991 the story of the abduction of a young woman with Down's Syndrome, Jo Ramsden, became national news. She went missing during a short walk from her day centre to a leisure centre where she regularly helped to set up equipment for a toddler's group. A psychiatric nurse was charged with her kidnapping. Although admitting five kidnappings, three rapes and one attempted rape, involving women with learning disabilities, he was not convicted of kidnapping Jo Ramsden.

Whilst the story of Jo Ramsden is well-known, there remains little general awareness of other attempted abductions. How often do men try to pick up women with learning disabilities? One woman, who tells how she was asked to get into a car and go to the pub, complied, but then panicked and jumped out. Another woman recounts that when she was standing at a bus stop a man said,

> 'I fancy you love. Come and have a cup of tea.'

She now dislikes waiting for buses and is afraid, at night, that the last bus may be cut out, leaving her stranded.

Abductions are not restricted to women. One man reports a sexual assault after being picked up and taken to a flat by two (female) prostitutes. Before this he relates how he was taken to his own flat which was ransacked, and his sound system disappeared. They also found a bank book, took him to a bank and forced him to withdraw around £1000. He was then forced to buy drugs with the money. Although his description of the prostitutes' flat was accurate, and his pen was found behind a sofa cushion, the Crown Prosecution Service (CPS) would not proceed with a prosecution. Reportedly, this was in part because of doubts about the possibility of women sexually assaulting a man.

Staff sacked over patient tied to toilet

David Brindle
Social Services correspondent

SEVEN hospital managers and nursing staff have been sacked or disciplined over the death of a profoundly mentally handicapped woman who was left tied to a toilet while nurses went to lunch.

Among those held responsible is the manager of the hospital, the Stallington at Blythe Bridge, Staffordshire, who has been moved to another job and will not have his contract renewed in the spring... Miss Latham, who was 42, had been in the Stallington since the age of four.

She died in May after being tied to the inlet pipe of a toilet cistern by the ties of a bib placed round her neck. A nurse returned to her once to give her medication, and her body was found 45 minutes later by a cleaner... George Stevenson, Labour MP for Stoke-on-Trent South, which borders the Stallington, said the hooking-on practice had been 'horrific, degrading and tragic.'

Responsibility should be taken by management at the highest level.

The Guardian, 11 December 1992

3

This story exemplifies how specific laws fail in relation to the victimization facing people with learning disabilities in the modern world.

Concerning abduction, the Sexual Offences Act 1956 has three obvious shortcomings:

1. **It does not include the abduction of men.**
2. **It assumes that all people with learning disabilities are in 'the possession' of a guardian, and so, for example, may exclude abduction from a flat or other form of independent living.**
3. **It omits the possibility of abduction for sexual offences between women.**

These shortcomings clearly derive from the outdated world view underlying the legislation.

Men and women tell stories which could amount to an attempted abduction, but their perception of events is often unclear. Are people with learning disabilities taught to recognise attempted abduction? Do they know to report such incidents, and do they know how helpful it is to remember details like car colour and what the person looked like? Are reports taken seriously? Even at the period of the Jo Ramsden abduction, police in an adjacent county apparently showed little interest in pursuing a similar case. **Recognising and dealing with abduction attempts should be a key element in personal safety training, for women and men.**

> It is an offence...for a person to take a woman who is a defective out of the possession of her parent or guardian against his will, if she is so taken with the intention that she shall have unlawful sexual intercourse with men or a particular man.
>
> Sexual Offences Act 1956 s21 (1)

Assault and battery

Assault in public places seems a significant problem. A London man relates how he was walking down the road and a group of drunken men shouted,

> 'What the bloody hell are you following us for. We'll do you over if you follow us.'

The man was then punched in the mouth and ended up in hospital, needing stitches. Another man was knocked unconscious when he offered help to a neighbour who seemed to be in distress, but turned out to be drunk and violent.

Robbery is a common motive for assault. Six youths demanded money from a man as he walked home from his girlfriend's house. He was kicked, punched and beaten around the head with a stick. The assailants made off with £15 and the victim needed eight stitches for facial injuries that doctors concluded 'could not have been caused simply by thumping'. Standard 'muggings' are also reported, often in full view of passers-by, with victims losing handbags, bumbags, walkmans and anything that it appears possible to grab.

YOBS ATTACK SICK ANGLER

A DISABLED and nearly-deaf angler almost drowned after two laughing yobs pushed him into a fast-flowing river.

Mentally handicapped Simon Ward, 37, was swept 60 yards by the swirling icy current until brave fishing rival Andy Palmer jumped in and dragged him out.

The two teenage thugs sneaked up behind Simon, who lives with his parents in Salisbury, Wilts. Then they bundled him into the nearby River Avon. They cackled as the angler – weighed down by boots and clothing – shouted for help and swallowed water.

Daily Star, 22 February 1993

There seem remarkably few reports of victimizers exploiting obvious physical vulnerability. In one of the rare instances a 'down-and-out' attacked a woman, who was part of a group, holding her by the throat and demanding money. The woman was described as small and obviously vulnerable because she was wearing built-up medical shoes. The reason that physical disability does not seem to attract attention is probably very simple: people with learning disabilities and mobility problems are usually accompanied when out on the streets.

Minor assaults in care settings are daily events in the lives of many service users. Pinching is common between people with learning disabilities, but how many men are taught that pinching a woman's bottom could get them a criminal record for indecent assault? A four-inch bruise, apparently from a bite, on the arm of one woman was not entered in the day centre's accident book, parents were not advised, and there was apparently no consideration of police involvement. It is only necessary to sit in a magistrates' court for a morning to learn that, in other settings, the same injury might have led to a charge of Grievous Bodily Harm and compensation of around £75.

From observing staff behaviour in care settings it seems clear that many are unaware that any form of touching, without consent, might be a common assault. This could include staff pulling or pushing people in a direction they do not want to go. There is a clear difference between taking someone's hand and leading him or her willingly to the dinner table, and pulling someone by the hand who is unwilling to move. Pushing, using arm locks, and pulling by the ears or hair, are more extreme examples of assaults by staff.

Traffic offences

Injury resulting from traffic is rarely considered as victimization. As people with learning disabilities are frequent pedestrians, they are front-line victims of bad driving. Rarely is there any redress. The victim of a hit-and-run driver in the West of England was not even visited by police because they considered, without meeting him, that he would not be able to say what had happened. One man reported nearly being run over on a pedestrian crossing by a driver who shouted at him, 'You fool!' The car was a police car.

Sexual offences

Sexual victimization is the one area of crime that has received significant attention from researchers, professionals and police both in the UK (see Dunne and Power 1990; Brown and Craft 1992; BIMH 1992; Craft 1992; Ridout 1993) and abroad (see Tharinger, Horton and Milea 1990; Senn 1988; Roeher 1992).

An assault is any act committed intentionally or recklessly, which causes another person to apprehend immediate and unlawful personal violence... There seems no logical reason why mere words should not amount to an assault...[and similarly] compulsion, a threatening gesture or a threat to use violence... [In one case] staring through a window at night, intending to frighten an elderly occupant of a room, constituted assault despite the physical barrier between accused and victim

Halsbury's Laws Vol 11, para. 488

An excellent annotated bibliography about sexual abuse and learning disabilities is available from

NAPSAC
Department of Learning Disabilities
Floor E, South Block
University of Nottingham Medical School
Queens Medical Centre
Nottingham
NG7 2UH

Like the pattern of concern about the victimization of children, 'sexual abuse' has preceded a more general awareness of crime against people with learning disabilities.

Existing research suggests a bias towards offences in service settings. This is not surprising as much of the research is, for practical reasons, carried out in this environment. Nevertheless, it seems clear that one of the most dangerous places, as far as sexual crime is concerned, is a care setting.

Whilst staff obviously have a general knowledge of common law sexual offences, they are less often aware that the law can specifically support prosecution when victims have severe learning disabilities (in legal terms, 'mental defects'). There is on-going discussion about this area of legislation, particularly Section 7 of the Sexual Offences Act 1956 (see Ridout 1993: 57 and Ashton and Ward 1992: 114). This disallows unlawful sexual relations with someone with severe learning disabilities, yet permits the defence that the perpetrator did not know that a victim was thus labelled. The law is clearly problematic when trying to permit a person with learning disabilities normal, consenting sexual relations. In Canada the offence of having sexual intercourse with a woman with mental handicap was removed from the Criminal Code in 1983.

The use of sexual offences legislation within the Mental Health Act 1959, is often not considered if the offence did not take place in a hospital, yet it directly covers staff as perpetrators. Group homes run directly by Health Services are almost certainly covered by the Act; sub-contracted arrangements would also seem to be included. **The Act should be amended to include sexual assault and sexual offences by female staff.**

Even less well known is an aspect of the Sexual Offences Act which makes those responsible for running any establishment guilty of an offence if they 'knowingly' let a woman with severe learning disabilities have sexual intercourse with a man. One of the disabilities this law creates is that it may deter reporting of a sexual offence by house managers, who might fear that it could be shown that they were aware of unlawful sexual relations.

On a less serious level, indecent exposure seems quite common, especially on buses. In one instance it was accompanied by the man threatening the woman with a bottle. One taxi driver exposed himself to a woman who was a regular customer of the firm. Although the police were not involved, for fear of further traumatizing the woman, the firm concerned instantly dismissed the driver, and the woman was at least aware that some form of justice had been achieved. **The law concerning indecent exposure has a weakness that is specific to the lives of people in care settings – it only relates to exposure in a public place or if the act can be seen from a public place.**

Reports of sexual assault usually contain three elements:

- the relative power of the perpetrator over victim and others who may report suspicious behaviour;

- the ability of the perpetrator to create or take advantage of the isolation of the victim;

- the difficulty of reporting.

These three factors should form the basis for discussing safer environments for people who are potentially at risk.

it shall be an offence
(b)   for a man to have unlawful sexual intercourse with a woman who is a mentally disordered patient and who is subject to his guardianship under this Act or is otherwise in his custody or care under this Act...or as a resident in a residential home for mentally disordered persons...

Mental Health Act 1959 s128 (1) (a)

It is an offence for a person who is the owner or occupier of any premises, or who has, or acts or assists in, the management or control of any premises, to induce or knowingly suffer a woman who is a defective to resort to or be on those premises for the purpose of having unlawful sexual intercourse with men or a particular man.

Sexual Offences Act 1956 s27 (1)

A member of staff who exposed himself or herself to a resident in a garden shed of a group home, for example, may not be guilty of an indecent exposure offence at common law.

It is interesting to note how the Sexual Offences Act 1956 relates to prostitution. It is hard to explain why this section refers to 'anywhere in the world', and the assumption is that only women can be prostitutes. In contrast, the prosecution of staff who sexually assault service users when they are on holiday in other countries is at present virtually impossible. Legislation framed in the manner of this part of the Sexual Offences Act could remedy this situation.

Serious sexual assaults are not restricted to women. In one instance a man was allegedly 'black and blue', and had a detached retina, from being thrown back into his wheelchair after sexual assaults by junior staff which were watched through a window by their managers. Men are sometimes in settings that make them particularly vulnerable. In Swindon a 15-year-old boy with autism was sexually assaulted after being lured to a pub by someone he met at a football match. Men are probably more likely to be on the streets alone. In one case a serious sexual assault took place near a man's flat when he was returning from the fish and chip shop. There are instances of female prostitutes regularly selling their services to men with learning disabilities in flats without live-in staff. The degree to which this may be exploitative, sexually or financially, is very hard to discern.

The outcomes of sexual victimization against men may also, in part, be gender-specific. Following a sexual assault in the street, the victim became very upset and obsessive about washing himself. He was previously confident and very capable, but became afraid to go out. His family were very upset, which was compounded by their horror at what they saw as the homosexual nature of the attack.

Men are not the primary concern of existing legislation. Not least, the rape of men is not clearly acknowledged. The Sexual Offences Act 1967 makes homosexual acts with a 'defective' illegal, but existing legislation can make healthy, consenting relationships unlawful. Homosexual acts between men in their own homes, may be illegal under the Sexual Offences Act 1967 s1(1) because they may not be 'in private' if there is a 'likelihood of a third person coming upon the scene'. The failure of a service provider to put a lock on an individual's bedroom door could create this circumstance.

There is one very unique aspect of sexual offences concerning women with learning disabilities. Often the basis of a request by parents that a daughter with learning disabilities should be sterilized, is the fear of rape and a resultant pregnancy. In the past this was accepted with little questioning. Fortunately judges are now recognizing the illogicality of effectively sanctioning an assault (i.e. operation) on a women because of a crime a man might commit against her.

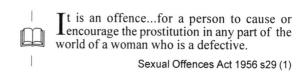

It is an offence...for a person to cause or encourage the prostitution in any part of the world of a woman who is a defective.

Sexual Offences Act 1956 s29 (1)

In a recent case a judge went so far as to point out that a sterilization may *increase* the chances of rape, because of lessened vigilance by carers.

Legislation concerning sexual relations and people with learning disabilities clearly needs reviewing. In its present form the law:

> **relies greatly on the term 'mental defect' which is vague, inappropriate and offensive. The phrase 'a person who, because of intellectual disabilities, cannot consent' would be more appropriate and is in line with current work, concerning mental incapacity, by the Law Commission**

> **can make healthy, consenting relationships unlawful**

> **could deter the reporting of sexual offences**

> **is gender-biased in a way that does not reflect what is now known about sexual offences against men**

> **reflects an outdated view of the lives of people with learning disabilities – most legislation was conceived before community care and 'normalization' principles.**

> **does not embrace offences committed in other countries except, curiously, those concerning the prostitution of women**

'Threatening, abusive or insulting words or behaviour' – in a public place

Verbal abuse is probably the most frequent form of victimization suffered by people with learning disabilities, in the streets. Being called names such as, 'spastic', 'cretin' and 'imbecile' is a daily event in many people's lives. Names related to obvious disabilities, such as 'blindy' or 'hop-along', are also common. The perpetrators are frequently children. 'Disabilist abuse' is often combined with racial abuse. A black employee relates how he had to leave his job: 'People used to call me things like "wog" and "coon".' Unless direct verbal abuse causes the victim to fear violence, it is not unlawful. Racial insults only constitute a specific offence if they incite racial hatred.

The part of the Public Order Act 1986 s4 relating to the fear 'that immediate unlawful violence will be used' is very relevant to the victimization of people with learning disabilities. In one case a group of youths leaving a pub demanded of a young man, just for fun, 'Let's have your money or we'll beat you up.' There are less obvious examples. One man who had regularly been generous towards 'gypsies' who were begging locally, but then decided to say 'No', became very afraid to find them sitting waiting outside his house during the course of one weekend. A woman who complained of a lack of police response

A person is guilty of an offence if he...uses towards another person threatening, abusive or insulting words or behaviour...with intent to cause that person to believe that immediate unlawful violence will be used against him or another by any person...or whereby that person is likely to believe that such violence will be used...

Public Order Act 1986 s4 (1)

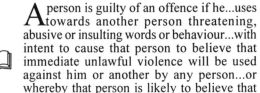

I was going to a shop round the corner and ten lads in a gang started winding me up by calling me names. I was frightened and went into a shop, but they waited round the corner. If I had a dog with me I don't think they would do it, but I don't have a dog.

to her phone call, reports,

> 'I was alone at home at night and these boys came in the garden and started running round the house. I'm still very upset about it.'

It is also worth noting the specific mention of missiles in the Public Order Act. People report tins thrown from buses, missiles such as coins, nails and cigarettes, and being drenched with high powered water pistols.

Sexual harassment (if not amounting to an assault) of women or men could amount to a Public Order offence if the victim feared immediate violence as a result. A report of sexual harassment against a man is easily overlooked. Whilst the comment,

> 'A man tried to touch my private parts in the toilet'

received instant attention from care workers, a man who simply said

> 'These girls kiss me'

had to repeat this a number of times before further enquiries were made. In this instance, the man had been sexually harassed on a bus, by schoolgirls shouting,

> 'What's that in your pocket? What have you got there? Or ain't you got one. Give it to us. Let's have a look.'

It is hard to excuse the placement of people with learning disabilities in living accommodation in areas known for a high incidence of Public Order offences. In one town the flats provided by social services for people with learning disabilities were in such a problematic area that the service advised its own social workers not to visit at night. In another area a housing association has found it necessary to close a large number of group homes because of the victimization of the residents.

Although Public Order offences are the most common form of victimization reported by people with learning disabilities, not one instance of a prosecution is known. A greater awareness of the Act is necessary amongst professionals and family carers, and there should be an insistence that police make use of Public Order legislation.

If the Public Order Act is more widely used concerning victims with learning disabilities, one difficulty will become apparent. Technically, the Act does not cover offences within a 'dwelling'. Therefore, the staff member who shouted to a resident,

'violence'... is not restricted to conduct causing or intended to cause injury or damage but includes any other violent conduct (for example, throwing at or towards a person a missile of a kind capable of causing injury which does not hit or falls short)...

Public Order Act 1986, s8

> 'Come here, you cretin. I'm going to hit you harder than you've ever been hit before.'

committed a Public Order offence because he did it in a local park. But had he said the said the same thing in the man's bedroom, the Public Order Act would not apply (although the behaviour would probably constitute an assault). But what if the incident happened in the garden of the man's group home?

A 'part of a structure' not 'occupied as a person's home or as other living accommodation' comes under the Public Order Act. Therefore garages, gardens, and sheds may be included. It seems very probable that quasi-public areas such as staff rooms and offices would also be included, but this has not been tested. If a victim ran from a garden to staff room to a bedroom during the course of a single incident, the arguments in court could be very complex. The importance is that numerous offences causing people to fear violence happen in exactly these areas.

The extent to which the Public Order Act applies to the quasi-public areas of group homes needs to be clarified, because the Act was conceived before deinstitutionalization and community care legislation created new forms of 'dwelling'.

Threatening, abusive or insulting words or behaviour – in a dwelling.

The ambiguity of the Public Order Act leads to the question, how does the law relate to the same type of victimization *inside* a dwelling? The question is important because of the unique constitution of a group home: a 'dwelling' which is a home to some of the occupants, but may be a workplace for others. This may lead to forms of victimization that sit comfortably within the intent of Public Order legislation, but are outside its current remit.

In circumstances in which Public Order legislation is inapplicable other laws can help, principally common assault. A strength of the Public Order legislation is that it clearly relates to threatening actions where no physical contact takes place, so it is very important to remember that a common assault does not necessarily entail contact. A graphic example was the case of Sydney Kang, the Vietnamese man who fired a starting pistol in the vicinity of Prince Charles during his 1994 visit to Australia. Although there was no physical contact, the charge was assault because obviously the Prince would have feared violence.

The concept of ill-treatment or wilful neglect, within the Mental Health Act 1983 s127 is another legal framework for overcoming the ambiguous legal position of residential settings. It is usually not considered that managers and staff, who are not directly employed by the NHS, may still be working within the Mental Health Act, if they are sub-contracted by a Health authority. The terms 'in-patient' and 'mental disorder' used in the Act are defined very widely, and almost certainly embrace people with learning disabilities in community settings (see Gunn 1990:18). Service providers contracted by the NHS to provide residential care, are probably operating a 'mental nursing home' on behalf of the NHS and are therefore also probably covered by the Act. The Registered Homes Act 1984 s22 further defines 'mental nursing home'.

The importance is that it would be far easier to obtain a conviction for borderline offences, especially neglect, under the Mental Health Act than through other criminal or civil law, and the sanctions may well be greater because of the clear breach of trust. For example, charges were brought against nursing staff in Colchester, of 'wilful neglect', for failing to attend to a badly cut lip, and of 'ill-treatment' for ridiculing a woman.

The degree to which the Mental Health Act 1983 s127, concerning ill-treatment or wilful neglect, relates to settings that are not designated a health service 'hospital or home', although the individuals concerned are under health service care, needs to be clarified.

The Registered Homes Act 1984 provides another route for dealing with victimization within a home. Homes can be closed 'urgently' by application to a single magistrate, or by a Registered Homes Tribunal. The Act seems to relate particularly well when abusive punishments have been used. For example in an instance where '...sanctions employed by the staff included depriving service users of their dessert. On one occasion a man was made to watch others eating their Easter eggs while he was denied his.' (*Nursing Standard* 1992: 51)

(1) It shall be an offence for any person who is an officer on the staff or otherwise employed in, or who is one of the managers of, a hospital or mental nursing home – (a) to ill-treat or wilfully to neglect a patient for the time being receiving treatment for mental disorder as an in-patient in that hospital or home; or (b) to ill-treat or wilfully to neglect, on the premises on which the hospital or home forms part, a patient for the time being receiving such treatment there as an out-patient.

(2) It shall be an offence for any individual to ill-treat or wilfully to neglect a mentally disordered patient who is for the time being subject to his guardianship under this Act or otherwise in his custody or care (whether by virtue of any legal or moral obligation or otherwise)...

Mental Health Act 1983 s127

URGENT CANCELLATION OF REGISTERED HOMES STATUS
A Justice of the Peace may make an urgent order cancelling the registration of a Registered Home, if it appears to the Justice of the Peace that there will be a serious risk to the life, health or well-being of the residents in the home unless the order is made...

Registered Homes Act 1984 11 (1) (b)

False imprisonment

False imprisonment is common in the lives of people with learning disabilities. Although clearly a common law offence, the police rarely make charges under false imprisonment. Some instances of serious deprivation of liberty have been reported. One local radio station reported how young boys apparently kept a man captive in his own house for two days, taunting him and burning him with cigarettes. Abductions will inevitably entail false imprisonment. Again, care settings seem the most usual arena for imprisonment offences. In one residential home a student witnessed residents being dragged along by their hair and locked in their rooms by brooms wedged against door handles:

On a number of occasions I witnessed service users being 'boxed in' as an off-the-cuff response to their negative behaviour. They were hauled into the lobby area and all three doors were shut. They hated it. Some of them had banged holes into the lobby's plasterboard walls with their heads while they were incarcerated there.

Report from a voluntary community home for people with autism,
Nursing Standard, 6,39,17 June 1992: 50

False imprisonment could include preventing someone leaving a room by wedging the door shut with a chair, tying a garden gate shut, but also simply telling someone to stay in a room under threat. Any imprisonment by physical means would also probably contravene fire regulations. 'Punishments' such as keeping people in their pyjamas to prevent them leaving, and curfews ('You must be back by 10 o'clock or I will lock you out') may also be false imprisonment because of the compulsion element.

Staff often 'imprison' people spontaneously, without realizing that **any** deprivation of liberty is illegal unless covered by the Mental Health Act or done in an emergency to prevent injury or damage. Often people are told to stay in a room because they 'have been naughty' or 'to get you out of harm's way'. Even in emergency situations, keeping people in a room for more than a few minutes has led to the closure of registered homes and staff dismissals.

Managers often fail to see the importance of enforcing the law concerning false imprisonment. One of the most striking reminders of the consequences of an 'OK, but don't let me see you do it' attitude was the death of a woman who was left hooked to a lavatory by her bra straps (see p.3). This was not an act of aggression nor a failure of duty to care in the eyes of the staff – it was a regular happening accepted by everyone. But had they had an awareness of the law of 'false imprisonment' this might have led to them questioning their practice before it became fatal.

Theft and robbery

By comparison to the general population, property offences appear a less significant problem for people with learning disabilities – they usually have very little valuable property. But this is a statistical view. Whilst people with learning disabilities may less often suffer loss through theft, and the losses may be smaller, the effects on the lives of victims can be significant. A man who had his bus pass stolen was effectively immobilized for three weeks until he had saved the money for a replacement. Another man, who lives on his own and was burgled, lost his radio and record player and all his food. As this was on a Saturday evening it was only thanks to sympathetic police officers that he did not go hungry.

Robbery sometimes seems related to perceived vulnerability. A man who had his bumbag stolen outside a London train station was first pushed against a wall and called 'spastic'. The assailant got away with £4. His mother concluded,

> 'This boy was just taking advantage of the situation like others do with elderly people. They hit out at those who can't fight back because they are vulnerable in some way.'

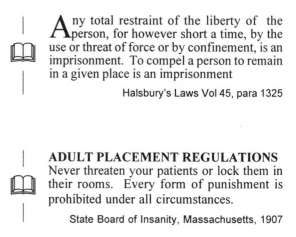

Any total restraint of the liberty of the person, for however short a time, by the use or threat of force or by confinement, is an imprisonment. To compel a person to remain in a given place is an imprisonment

Halsbury's Laws Vol 45, para 1325

ADULT PLACEMENT REGULATIONS
Never threaten your patients or lock them in their rooms. Every form of punishment is prohibited under all circumstances.

State Board of Insanity, Massachusetts, 1907

A friend commented in a similar manner,

> 'He is so loving, but he is vulnerable and it just makes me sick that this could happen to such a nice person.'

But 'vulnerability' can be overstated – *anyone* can be vulnerable. It is the power of the perpetrator, enhanced by the context of the event that is the cause for concern. Certainly the attacker was aware of his relative strength in this case, but why was this robbery possible in a crowded London street, outside a railway station, in the middle of the day?

When residential homes are burgled it is common that the victim is seen as the home owner rather than the residents. Apart from the obvious need for justice, felt by all victims, staff are sometimes unaware that they may be bound by the Registered Homes Act 1984. This includes a duty to notify the registration authority within 24 hours of 'any event in the home which affects the well-being of any resident; and any theft, burglary...' In many cases, service providers only include the property of the organization within insurance policies. In one case a residential home was reimbursed for a stolen TV, but residents who lost walkmans, watches and clocks of a much greater total value received nothing. **The insurance policies of service providers should include the property of residents, if that is what they wish.**

Deception

Deception is a hidden but seemingly widespread aspect of financial abuse. What exactly is happening between the young man and his 'girlfriend', a woman whom he met at his local pub and who, 'always gets me to pay for things'? It can be difficult to decide when a few instances of 'taking advantage' becomes a pattern of serious exploitation.

Police sometimes seem reluctant to pursue cases when someone exploits the intellectual naivety of a person with learning disabilities. Presumably this is because they consider that someone they see as 'vulnerable' has contributed to their own victimization. In one example, although the police attended the incident quickly, and interviewed a suspect, their general attitude was questionable:

> 'The police made it quite clear that they were not pleased that the victim had been allowed to go to the Post Office without a member of staff. They said, 'People in his condition are vulnerable and should not be allowed out on their own.'

> *He went to the Post Office to collect his pension. A young girl [around 16] who was waiting outside told him she was his friend and told him to give her his money and she would buy him a bike and bring it to him at the hostel later on. He was found by a member of staff, standing outside Spar shop, looking up the road expecting to see the girl bringing the bike. He will not now collect his pension on his own without staff and is still expecting this girl to bring him a bike. [Following a newspaper report of the story, he received cheques totalling £200 from local people].*

13

If this logic is to be applied to crime prevention generally, women should never go out alone after dark, no one should ever open a front door to strangers, and people should not leave valuable things, like cars, unattended. 'Blaming the victim' should be consistent or not be part of any police response.

A difficult circumstance arises when theft appears to involve a breach of trust by someone with a duty to care. In one instance around £2000 disappeared from a young man's building society account, despite the precaution of his parents setting up one small account with easy access and a main one for which the book was kept locked up. Staff at the building society concerned remembered the young man often going in with another man – they were cheerful and there was no sign of duress. The parents discovered that a staff member from the man's home, 'with whom he had a really good rapport', was in hospital with a breakdown; that he was in serious financial disabilities and (anecdotally) that one of the other residents had also lost money. There was also mention of a threat of suicide from the suspect to the victim, if the truth was revealed, and that the victim perhaps 'bought friendship' on other occasions when small amounts of money disappeared. It was decided, with the police, to take no further action because the evidence was unclear and the victim was distressed at the idea of a court case.

> *People had spotted their vulnerability and abused their good nature. Julie used a catalogue from which others would order and not pay for their goods. Neighbours borrowed money and equipment and failed to return or repay it. Their gas meter was broken into; other women made use of Julie's washing machine; distant relatives lodged with them without contributing to their own keep. Even her stepfather tapped them for loans. Eventually things caught up with them. They defaulted on their gas bill, were fined for not having a TV licence and had their TV and video repossessed.*

Wendy and Tim Booth, December 1992

Damage

Again, as people with learning disabilities own very little property, criminal damage is not frequently mentioned as a cause of concern. There are occasional reports, by individuals, of windows broken by stones, and washing lines cut and washing stolen or ruined. But the buildings in which people live communally and those which they attend during the day are frequently damaged, not least in attempts to steal sound systems, TVs and videos. Arson, broken windows (especially of greenhouses) and graffiti are common problems. In one case superb Gaudiesque mosaic sculptures in a garden, a year's work by the members of one day centre, were wrecked in one night by young vandals.

The important point, as with theft, is that the victim of damage to buildings is usually seen as the owner (e.g. the Health or Social Services, or housing associations) and not the residents or users. Consequently the usual victim support mechanisms are not made available, yet the trauma, annoyance, and sense of injustice may be just as great as for more direct victimization.

Sometimes staff may also suffer victimization because of their job. In one incident staff cars were damaged, so too was the car of a neighbour known to be sympathetic to the opening of a new group home in a neighbourhood that was otherwise antagonistic.

Incitement and complicity

Stories about people with learning disabilities who are encouraged to offend by others are very difficult to verify. Teachers at one special school complain that their older pupils are sometimes encouraged to break windows or steal things from gardens by known gangs in the neighbourhood.

The motive for these incidents seems more a matter of sport than financial gain, but they can lead to more serious exploitation. There are reports of people becoming involved with soft drugs, and being used to distribute illegal substances.

The problem of incitement may not only come from the community. In one case a male nurse was sacked for inciting a male resident to make sexual advances towards a woman resident.

It is an indictable offence at common law for a person to incite or solicit another to commit an offence, even though no such offence is either committed or attempted.

Halsbury's Laws Vol 11 (1) para 58

Victimization before adulthood

When considering adult victims, it is easy to overlook events in childhood that have life-long outcomes. For some, victimization may be a cause of learning disabilities; for others, victimization in childhood leaves lasting scars.

Civil claims because of brain damage resulting from medical negligence are becoming more successful, but it is necessary to establish liability by the health authority and to prove that a negligent action by hospital staff caused the injury. Initial legal aid is limited and the cost of preliminary investigations, reviewing medical records and getting counsel's opinion, is often prohibitive. The bases for the settlement can be erratic. In one case a child from a wealthy legal family was awarded £1.2 million against a negligent health authority on the grounds that he was 'physically attractive and with artistic and entrepreneurial genes in his ancestry' (*The Independent,* 22 December 1990: 6).

Recently a Court of Appeal ruling confirmed that a child disabled by pre-natal injury, an 'unborn victim', *can* sue for damages. (*B v Islington Health Authority; D v Merton and Sutton Health Authority,* 18 March 1992). The ruling would apply to medical negligence, but also in other circumstances such as negligence in respect of a train or a motor vehicle in which a pregnant mother was travelling.

In 1992, a woman who kicked a pregnant neighbour in the stomach, causing brain damage to the foetus from which it died, was charged with manslaughter – the first case of its kind (*Guardian* 15 May 1992: 2). This raises many questions. Can a foetus be the direct victim of a criminal assault?

15

Might a foetus be awarded compensation in criminal assault cases? The Criminal Injuries Compensation Board has confirmed that an unborn victim would be eligible. Although no payments have been made, a recent decision held,

> 'We accept that 'personal injuries' is a term which can properly be applied to injuries occurring before birth and do not regard the precise stage at which injuries occured as relevant to our decision.'
>
> (*R* v *CICB* ex parte *P* 1993).

Negligent driving by expectant mothers is another aspect. A boy was awarded £700,000 by the High Court in Belfast, in this circumstance. This is thought to be the first case of its kind under the Congenital Disabilities (Civil Liability) Act 1976. In a similar case a mother was ordered by a court in Sydney to pay £1.3 million damages .

In the US, foetal alcohol syndrome is now the 'leading known cause of mental retardation', and in 1986 9202 infants were born with indications of maternal drug use. Mothers are now being charged with 'distributing' drugs to their unborn child. (Berger 1991: 4). However, in the UK the Congenital Disabilities (Civil Liability) Act 1976, whilst specifying brain damage caused by an expectant mother's negligent driving and attempting to redress injury from environmental factors such as radiation, excludes claims in relation to abuse of drugs and alcohol. **The Congenital Disabilities Act 1976 could usefully be revised in the light of American experience, increased scientific knowledge about *in utero* damage, and the growth of the drug culture since the time the legislation came into being.**

Victimization in infanthood provides another part of the picture. One man's intellectual injury stems from him surviving, as a child, a family suicide attempt, through the use of gas. Yet he is not seen by anyone around him as being the victim of a crime. In a more recent case a man, who shook a neighbour's 22-month-old daughter 'so violently that she was brain damaged and crippled', was jailed for three years and nine months after being found guilty of assault and grievous bodily harm. (*Guardian*, 12 May 1992: 2). Again, people with a specific duty to care feature as perpetrators.

Children are not only at risk during infancy. Negligent driving is a significant threat to older children.

Disability resulting from vaccine damage is probably the most contentious aspect of childhood brain injury. The Vaccine Damage Payments Act 1979 was intended to redress the situation, but it is not a helpful piece of legislation. Four out of five claimants under the 1979 Act fail to gain compensation, because of its complexity and interpretation. Not least this is because access to medical records can lawfully be withheld *under the regulations to the 1979 Act.*

A woman whose son suffered brain damage while being cared for by a council-approved childminder, suspected of injuring another child in her care, won her claim for damages. The childminder was held liable to pay damages to Thomas, aged four, who sustained injuries which have left him brain damaged and partially sighted, while he was in her care. His injuries are believed to have been the result of being severely shaken.

The council was held liable for failing to tell the boy's mother that there was a question mark over [the child minder] after another child she had looked after suffered similar injuries three months earlier...

No damages were claimed on behalf of the first child, though the judge ruled that his injury, which left him with epileptic seizures, learning disabilities and behavioural problems, was non-accidental

Guardian 21 January 1994: 2

A 12-year-old boy who suffered severe brain damage after being hit by a speeding motorcyclist was yesterday awarded more than £1 million damages.

John became aggressive and hyperactive after the accident nine years ago.

His mother described having to cope with her son's disability. 'He hits me, bites me and pulls my hair out. I get him a skinhead haircut so he cannot pull his hair out.' John was unable to sleep properly and was prone to self mutilation.

Guardian 31 July 1991: 2

Thousands of claimants have failed because of 'lost records', or because the degree of damage is assessed as less than 'severe', that is less than 80% . Why are mild or moderate disabilities excluded, and *how* can the intellectual disability of a child be assessed in percentage terms in the same manner used for employment-related benefit? The Act limits payments to £30,000, yet a civil case concerning vaccine damage brought in the Republic of Ireland ended with a damages payment of £2.7 million. **The administration of the Vaccine Damage Payments Act 1979 should be reviewed urgently.**

Victimization in childhood is the final part of the picture of 'adult victimization'. Children with learning disabilities seem to suffer frequent victimization, according to American studies, to a greater degree than children without disabilities. In 1992, a teacher at a special school was accused of 32 offences, including forcing boys to have sex with him during swimming lessons and in bedrooms. One victim reported, 'I was frightened to tell anyone in case he beat me up. I saw him do the same thing with other boys' (*Guardian* 1992: 2). In the same year Lancashire County Council were criticised for not taking parents' complaints seriously concerning a school for autistic children. Staff had been smacking, pulling hair and forcing children to eat regurgitated food. There were 94 incidents of alleged ill-treatment (Sherratt 1992: 5). Children with disabilities are commonly bullied by others. Further examples of abuse are identified in *Abuse of children and adults with disabilities* (Westcott 1993), *Child protection work with children with multiple disabilities* (Marchant and Page 1992), and 'Bullying of children with special needs in mainstream schools' (Thompson, Whitney and Smith 1994).

A landmark civil action was taken, in 1994, by a young women with cerebral palsy who maintained that her school should have protected her from 'wilful and persistent abuse' by other pupils. Where do children get these attitudes? Adult examples such as that of the headmistress who asked publicly,

> 'What is this mongol person doing in any school?'

or the teacher who threatened a boy with Down's Syndrome:

> 'I'll hang you up on the washing line by your balls'

cannot help.

Lifelong victims

Most victim studies base their conclusions on an analysis of isolated incidents. Whilst studies may discover the incidence of specific crimes, the criminogenicity of various settings, or the propensity of certain groups to offend, they rarely reveal the cumulative nature of victimization in the lives of individuals. It is the stories of cumulative, individual victimization that most distinguishes the experience of people with learning disabilities: they are often lifelong victims. Events which may seem trivial in themselves, take on much greater significance when they all happen to the same person.

For information about vaccine damage, and support contact:

 Justice for All Vaccine Damaged Children UK

Erins Cottage
Fussells Buildings
Whiteway Road
St George
Bristol BS5 7QY

17

When I was at school, I won a first prize – the Observers' Book of Birds. *That got pinched, two years later. And my school cap went missing. I don't know if it was this girl or this boy who did it.*

Later, when I was away, I got kicked in the testicles, by someone who was on the same ward as me, up in Buckinghamshire. Then when I was at Hortham, somebody pinched my New Testament and Psalms.

In Liverpool, I can remember a councillor, a Conservative on the Liverpool Council, and he gave me two law books. Which I studied because I was interested in law – criminal and public law. They were in my locker. Just before I was moving, they went missing.

I was moved to a place like an open prison because I rebelled against Hortham. I was with this man from Rampton and they had to pin something on me. After about my sixth year out of twenty years in that place I lost a radio which had a brown case. It was grey with orange buttons. I never got the radio back. They said, 'You should look after your own stuff.' I don't know if it was a screw or an inmate. If it was a screw they would say, 'I bought it down the market.'

The screws kicked you in the gut. It wasn't just one, believe me, it was about six of the buggers. And you had to lie still and get more. The trouble is people let these things go by. They keep shut up about it, so it goes unnoticed. They're afraid what's been done to them will be done again if they're found out.

When I came out, I was in a house, and a resident poured boiling water over me for no reason at all. The next day I was in hospital. I was so dazed I didn't even know my own mother. The police came, but didn't do anything.

Then I moved. A woman there accused me of going into her bedroom. I have a letter that says this was not proved. But I was moved out back into a hospital. When I went there, three things went missing. I had a camera – that went missing. And I had a blue baseball cap which was took. We got it back, washed it and someone took it again. And an extension lead which I had for my television, that went missing. Three things went missing.

When I was a kid I had a vaccination. My doctor had never given this vaccine before. My mum says, after it I went funny and started blinking. The doctor gave my mother some pills and said report back in two weeks time. There were no records then. Everything was trying to be hush hush then.

I think I keep going because of letting my old man down. So I just have to battle on.

Especially written for this book by Peter Stevens, Bristol

2
CHAPTER

Who are the perpetrators?

Is there anything distinctive about the profile of the people who victimize? Motivation in individual cases is usually hard to assess, but it is possible to identify perpetrator *groups* whose relationship with the victims is, to a great extent, unique. These groups do not fit our preconceived ideas about 'criminals', and detection, effective prevention, and the achievement of justice are often hindered because of this. This lack of perpetrator recognition is a significant aspect of the 'invisibility' of victims with learning disabilities.

Professionals and staff

Sadly, professionals and general staff appear frequently as perpetrators. This should not be overstated because, for most people with learning disabilities, a large proportion of their lives is spent with 'staff', and reporting is likely to be higher than, for example, in family settings.

Often staff are affronted by the suggestion that they are a significant victimizer group. Good staff, the majority, are likely to be unaware of the actions of a minority – unaware of examples, such as one at a single group home, where the police have investigated 500 alleged incidents including assaults, withholding of medicines and locking residents in their rooms. Whatever the incidence rate, any victimization by a staff member is a serious breach of trust deriving from the very unequal power relationships involved in care settings.

Power relationships and exploitation are exemplified by the case in which the manager of a group home sexually assaulted a woman by hypnotising her.

EVIL SEX ATTACK HYPNOTIST JAILED

The manager of a home for handicapped people who hypnotised a woman to have sex with her has been jailed for seven years. Michael Murray was found guilty of rape and two offences of indecent assault on the woman...

The woman, who was partially deaf and partially sighted and of limited intellect, wept in the witness box as she told how Murray had used a pendulum to hypnotise her and ordered her to remove her clothes.

And she told how she woke to find she had been dressed again – but with her jumper the wrong way round.

Murray was able to put his victim into a trance using a pendulum made from the end of a bathroom light cord... He also said he used faith healing and hypnotism to help the woman with pain and anxiety...

Judge Mr Justice Hutchison told him: 'You abused the trust that was placed in you – you made spurious use of such powers of hypnotism as you possessed in order to overcome this woman's will.'

Evening Post (Bristol), 7 May 1992: 3

In other instances poor management is clearly a contributory factor. At Chelmsford a sexual assault was perpetrated by an odd-job man who had been promoted to 'social worker' at a private care home. An action that the trial judge commented, 'beggars belief.'

Many assaults are justified, by staff, in terms of 'control and restraint'. One dismissal resulted from a manager who, amongst other things, dragged a woman backwards with his arm around her neck, and shouted and swore at residents shouting abuse such as,

> 'You're a fucking animal – you're a fucking idiot.'

Whilst some incidents may be precipitated by difficult work conditions, others appear openly vindictive. A nurse in Colchester was dismissed for molesting a man by 'seizing his testicles or backside when he approached for help'. Another report tells how a man, who had been placed in a secure unit for exposing himself to girls in the park, was 'stripped naked and tied to a table and fellow residents and staff were encouraged to prod and abuse him verbally', because of the allegations against him.

In some settings a culture of victimization seems to develop. A report from a student led to parents discovering that residents at one home were dragged by their hair, locked in rooms by a broom pole wedged under the handle, and given food whilst sitting on the toilet. Staff at another home were alleged to have kissed, shouted at and locked up residents. One member of staff had to be prevented from putting a resident in a bath mixed with bleach and disinfectant.

The Mental Health Act 1983 specifically deals with abuse by staff in Health Service settings. Charges have been brought concerning a unit where,

> 'a severely handicapped 18-year-old was allegedly left to drip blood into his lunch after the charge sister refused to attend to his badly cut lip... He was left with the open wound all day...until the evening shift charge nurse arranged for him to go to hospital to have it stitched.'

> 'a nursing assistant threatened to wash out a screaming and sobbing mentally handicapped boy's mouth with soap as a punishment for swearing.'

> a nurse 'allegedly left a female patient alone in a bathroom of males and bathed them all in the same water.'

> staff 'laughed at and ridiculed a brain-damaged woman...after she wet herself.'

The senior personnel officer for the mental handicap unit concluded in court, 'I would say there was a feeling that training for nursing assistants was inadequate.'

Secret report alleges systematic abuse of handicapped adults

PK is a gentleman who is blind, as well as having a learning disability. Descriptions of assaults on him include *'Gordon lying in wait and pouncing'* and being deliberately dragged downstairs by the hair or ear and being deliberately pushed into furniture. He was often made to sit in a designated chair for days on end (one witness referred to two months) and belted around the head by Gordon Rowe whenever he went past. Being blind, he must have been in constant fear. Another person described how PK would be punched by Gordon Rowe as an 'example' to other residents. Yet another person described the physical injuries sustained by this blind gentleman when having been buggered by another resident. When PK was not being punished by sitting in the aforementioned chair by day, he would be in the classroom where he threaded beads – one person has told us he had been given nothing else to do for years.

Independent, 16 September 1994: 3

There are a few instances of Registered Homes status being withdrawn because of the level of victimization and abuse. In one case a Residential Homes Tribunal (Decision 218) mentioned: 'confining to rooms, shouting and anger expressed by the manager and his quick temper, the bullying, mocking and humiliation of residents, deprivation of food, deprivation of activity, smacking, punishments used to control residents which were 'misconceived and misleading'. One woman was 'sent to her room for about 15 minutes for wetting herself and playing up. She has even been denied underwear for wetting herself.' The 'institutional, authoritarian, restrictive and controlling regime at the home and the resulting fear and intimidation shown by residents' ended in the closure of the home, but only thanks to the efforts of citizen advocates who uncovered the abusive regime.

Staff unknowingly commit minor offences such as false imprisonment (when they confine people to their rooms), assault (when they touch people without their consent), and intercepting people's mail or incoming phone calls. One man, who was earning a considerable amount from a part time job, never had enough money to buy a paper or cup of tea because his pay cheque was always intercepted and banked by an over-enthusiastic residential manager.

Whilst doctors are usually very clear about the need for a patient's consent to treatment (unless in an emergency or covered by the Mental Health Act) this is sometimes overlooked when the patient has learning disabilities. Most service users cannot legally be compelled to undergo medical treatment, which would probably include minor treatments such as taking an aspirin, and certainly drugs to control behaviour. There is particular confusion concerning people who are transferred from long-stay hospitals, and are under Section 8 Guardianship Orders. Guardianship does not sanction compulsory treatment.

In one instance a home manager went to a GP and obtained tranquillizers for a resident, who he claimed was being aggressive, which were then given under threat of punishment. The manager was later dismissed for assaults and verbal abuse against residents, which was probably the cause of the behaviour problems.

Much physical abuse of people with learning disabilities has come under the guise of treatment or research. Globally the most disturbing case recently concerns the 62 'retarded' teenagers who were fed radioactive meals whilst at the Fernald State School (Waltham, US) as part of defence research.

Cruel nurse struck off

Enrolled nurse Andrew Chutter stuffed cotton wool balls into the mouth of a mentally handicapped female resident... after she refused medical treatment.

She was told: 'that's what you would look like if you had false teeth'...

He would also tip her wheelchair forwards while the resident was in it, for amusement; shouted at residents when they vomited or were incontinent... He pulled the hairs on the back of the legs of resident MD, and forcibly fed resident AD by pushing food into her mouth...

Western Gazette, 15 September 1994: 1

 ...a person who intentionally intercepts a communication in the course of its transmission by post or by means of a public telecommunication system shall be guilty of an offence...

Interception of Communications Act 1985, 1

A very thorough review of research practice by Guess *et al.* (in NDT 1993: 2) noted the use of physical restraint, electric shocks, pinching, slapping, pulling people's hair, cold water baths, spraying water at the face, white noise exposure up to 95 db, forced inhalation of ammonia fumes, lemon juice, vinegar or shaving cream forced into people's mouths. In North America a 22-year-old man died from 'treatment' during which he was shackled hand and foot, placed in a visual screening helmet, and exposed to white noise.

Whilst there seems to be a growing recognition that these practices are serious criminal acts (or should be), 'amateur' aversive treatment, by workers who have a rudimentary training in psychology, quite commonly includes deprivation of food and confinement to bedrooms. Acts that are taken as common behaviour modification practice by staff include telling people they cannot have a cup of tea because, 'You did not come on time' or because 'You've had two already.' The hospital mentality still pervades much staff practice.

Staff are usually not aware that they may be guilty of an offence if they impede a report to the police, if there is a suspect. Impeding a prosecution by omission (simply not reporting a crime) is not an offence. But any 'act' which intentionally impedes a prosecution may constitute an offence. The law has not been tested thoroughly in the context of community care. But a manager who, for example, instructs, verbally or in writing, that a probable crime should not be reported, may commit an offence. It is unlikely that a belief that the police will do nothing, that someone will be a bad witness, or fear of further traumatising a victim would be seen as a 'reasonable excuse'.

Similarly, staff are often unaware that to 'counsel' or 'incite' someone to commit an offence may itself be an offence. In one probable example, male staff decided that a woman 'needed a sexual relationship'. They arranged for her to have regular respite care where she was seduced by a resident known to be sexually very active. The staff may have committed an offence if the sexual advances were unwelcome or the woman was not able to give informed consent.

The level of staff awareness about minor victimization and the law is often very low. This problem is likely to increase as more reliance is put on the provision of residential care and other services by private agencies which often do not employ a high percentage of qualified staff. **If there is a single strategy that would reduce the amount of low-level victimization in the lives of people with learning disabilities, it is proper staff training about what constitutes an unlawful act.**

Impeding the apprehension or prosecution of arrestable offenders.

Where a person has committed an arrestable offence, any other person commits an offence who, knowing or believing him to be guilty of the offence or of some other arrestable offence, does, without lawful authority or reasonable excuse, any act with intent to impede his apprehension or prosecution.

Halsbury's Laws Vol 11 (1) para. 51

People with learning disabilities

The term 'challenging behaviour' can cloud the fact that incidents between people with learning disabilities are often technically offences. The difficulty is to acknowledge a victim's right to justice, along 'ordinary life' principles, whilst preventing an over-reaction against perpetrators who may not fully understand their actions. The feelings of a person who has been hit will be little different whether the perpetrator is a person with learning disabilities or a known criminal. Yet the outcomes, in these two different circumstances, for the victim, may be very different.

Offences are not always minor. Sexual assaults seem common in hospital settings, and often little attempt is made to investigate properly or ensure justice for the victim. In one case of aggravated rape, staff suggested that a related facial injury had been 'self-inflicted' – it was a bite. The police were informed, they 'ignored it largely', and the victim remains angry that she was not believed (except by one counsellor). Similar incidents happen in day centres.

Because people have learning disabilities other, more obvious, reasons for 'crime between intimates' are easily overlooked. In any walk of life, abuse between close friends or partners is all too common. One young woman relates in a very matter of fact way,

> 'I was hit by my boyfriend. He hit me and I fell on the ground. I don't go out with him any more. I didn't tell anyone. I still see him, but I don't go out with him.'

The closeness of the social world in which many people with learning disabilities must live, compounds the effects of peer victimization. Even a relatively minor incident, a woman being hit by a male resident at breakfast, led to her refusing to return home from her day centre and an on-going fear of being in a room with any man.

When sexual or physical assaults happen, it is very common for the victim to be moved to another house, disrupting life and friendships. Sometimes no action is taken. In one case a man is known to have previously assaulted at least four residents before being moved.

However, it can be equally inexcusable to move an alleged perpetrator if the allegations are not proven. In one case a man was accused by a female resident of entering her room and assaulting her. He denied this, but was moved immediately back into a long-stay hospital. He was threatened with the police, but they were never contacted. He later received a formal letter from the Health Service stating that the allegation was not proven.

*A resident poured boiling water over me for no reason at all. The next day I was in hospital. I was so dazed I didn't even know my own mother. But when I had got a bit better, my mother said, 'I will try and get compensation for you.' They said that seeing as the resident had learning disabilities, you cannot claim... Now if I had done something like that to someone **outside**, I would have been sent down.*

Sheffield social services is conducting an internal inquiry after a client with severe learning disabilities was accused by police of murdering a fellow resident at a special unit in the city... The two men were the sole occupants of the unit...police discovered the unit on fire, which caused extensive damage, and [X] was found dead. [Y] was subsequently charged and remanded to Hull prison...no unit staff were present during the alleged incident because they normally sleep in the adjoining hostel.

Community Care 16 January 1992: 3

The first question staff should ask in a situation such as this is very simple: what would we do if this man did not bear the label 'learning disabilities'? If an offence cannot be proven, no action can be taken against an alleged perpetrator, but alternatives can be offered to the victim. It is also worth considering that, in a court, a judgement of guilt is not based on a knowledge of previous convictions. Yet often staff base their assessment of guilt on a case file or anecdotal knowledge of a person's history. Similarly the police and courts would not maintain a formal record of allegations that were not proven. Staff might bear in mind that technically, an unsubstantiated verbal allegation that an individual had committed an offence could be slander. If the alleged offence was imprisonable the complainant would not have to prove loss to reputation or financial loss, so a claim would be relatively straightforward.

Another useful approach is to examine the dynamics which underlie a situation. Was there any *provocation* or *incitement*? Was the *intent* of the perpetrator unlawful? In Colchester, a nurse was dismissed for, amongst other things, inciting a male resident to make sexual advances to a woman resident. A Bristol woman recounts how she ended up in a police station cell because somebody she was with stole some butter and planted it in her shopping bag. The abused–abuser syndrome, now widely recognized in relation to child abuse, is argued lucidly, in an appropriate form, by Nigel Bull of London People First:

> 'If you feel people have the right to abuse your body, you feel you have the right to abuse other people's bodies.'

Some circumstances are far from straightforward. One social services department is concerned about increasing reports of sexual abuse, by parents with learning disabilities, of their children who also have learning disabilities. This is explained by a history of similar abuse against the parents when they were young which amounts to a 'learned way for parents to behave.'

In some circumstances it probably has to be accepted that victimizer–victim spirals are too interwoven for helpful analysis. Isabel Clare provides an example:

> 'Ms Jackson stole food from the communal kitchen and from other residents' plates...she was known to steal food from shops... On one occasion she returned home with bruises and her account indicated that she had been beaten and raped by a group of men. In the three years following her move into the home, she had accumulated at least 12 criminal convictions for shoplifting, criminal damage, and actual bodily harm.'

In such circumstances a move to a completely new location, 'a fresh start', if the person concerned agrees, may be the least problematic option.

> *You doing about crime? I did a crime – criminal damage. I kicked in two windows. I got taken to the police station and locked up in a cell. Then I got a caution.*
>
> *'Why did you do it?'*
>
> *This kid threw a cup of coffee over me and I got upset. But you can't take it out on a 12-year-old can you? So I took it out on the windows.*

When offences are between people with learning disabilities, police are sometimes happy to be told what to do. In one instance police were contacted by a woman with learning disabilities, because a friend from her day centre had stolen from her flat, when visiting. They discussed a strategy with the centre manager, and it was decided to interview the suspect. The woman admitted taking the money and was informally cautioned, stressing that she had committed an offence. It was then agreed by all parties that the money should be paid back at fifty pence per week. In another case, involving assault, the offender was similarly cautioned and then taken to see the police cells, with a reminder that he would find himself here if he did the same thing again. Unfortunately the police get very little credit for effective, but time-consuming work of this nature.

Police involvement has also proved successful in preventing potential offending. Staff at a group home became concerned that a man was expressing a strong desire to touch a woman sexually, in an unwelcome way. Following previous successful intervention by a community police officer, his help was enlisted. He warned the man of the possible consequences of touching the woman. The warning was taken very seriously.

If police are intending to charge someone with learning disabilities, they might be reminded (tactfully) of the possibility of cautioning. It is also acceptable to contact the CPS directly, although they may be unused to this. *In both cases the approach should not create the impression that there is any intent to influence the course of justice, simply to assist with the best possible decision.*

Guardianship under the Mental Health Act 1983 s37, is an underused option for offenders with learning disabilities, in part because it requires setting-up in a convincing manner before a case is heard in court. John was convicted following an incident when a single witness claimed that he took his trousers down whilst near a young child. He spent periods in prison, during which he was apparently sexually assaulted. Eventually a Guardianship Order was arranged and he ended up receiving a level of care that had never been available to him before. **If an offender with learning disabilities is likely to receive a custodial sentence, the probation service and defence solicitor should be reminded of the possibility of using a Guardianship Order (Mental Health Act 1983, s37).**

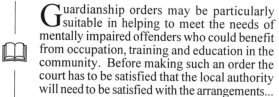

Guardianship orders may be particularly suitable in helping to meet the needs of mentally impaired offenders who could benefit from occupation, training and education in the community. Before making such an order the court has to be satisfied that the local authority will need to be satisfied with the arrangements...

Code of Practice: Mental Health Act 1983, HMSO (1993)

Children

Sadly children are commonly mentioned as perpetrators of low level victimization. One woman relates how she was walking in the park with her dog, and boys came along and hit her with branches, concluding simply,

> 'I don't go out with my dog any more.'

A People First group reported in their local paper,

> 'We don't think children really mean to be cruel... We get pushed about on buses and sometimes children stick chewing gum on our clothes, which is very hard to get off.' (Reported by Hilary Brook)

A number of people who live on their own report intimidation which includes bricks and stones thrown through windows.

Although relatively minor, such intimidation constantly impinges on daily lives. One psychologist remembers a client who was always late for appointments because she would take a variety of long routes between a bus stop and the clinic to avoid a school playground. An adult education project had to change its daily times so that the students could avoid victimization from pupils at a private, Catholic girls' school.

Victimization by children is not always against adults. The bullying of disabled children at school seems quite common. Nor is it just the disabled child who suffers. ChildLine reports of a child asking for their help because she was teased for having a 'brain-damaged sister' at a special school.

Incidents are not always minor. A London man tells how four 'kids' knocked at his door, forced their way into his flat and stole pictures and a baseball cap. More serious offences are not restricted to older children. One woman was assaulted and pushed to the ground by a group of primary school children, receiving injuries that would amount to actual bodily harm.

There is commonly a reticence to take action when children are perpetrators. There is a 'double disincentive' when conceptualizing an event as a crime – children are not readily seen as criminals and people with learning disabilities are not readily considered 'victims'. There are exceptions. A woman reports,

> 'I was mugged by two school girls. They has a knife. The caretaker where I lived called the police and they got them. I gave a statement. It took three-and-a-half hours because I was crying.'

It is worth examining more closely why children behave in this manner. Do they learn their attitudes from adults? A day

We were upstairs on the bus and some schoolkids started calling us 'dimwits' and everything. They said, 'Your breath smells – you smell.' They broke Mary's walkman and headphones. We got off the bus. Mary was crying. Janice was crying. They've been having a go at us ever since.

26

centre manager in Scotland notes, in connection with harassment by neighbours who do not want people with learning disabilities living in their road,

> 'Where I have found this by adults, is also the street where the children give the people with learning disabilities a hard time.'

Were the parents of children who constantly posted rubbish and excrement through the letterbox of their neighbours' house, where a woman with severe learning disabilities lived, completely unaware of what was happening?

The way in which people with learning disabilities conceptualize children is an important prerequisite of learning coping strategies. Nothing should be assumed. One woman who spent many years of social deprivation in a long stay hospital will admit publicly that, when she first moved into the community,

> 'I didn't know what children were. I really didn't. I thought they were all midgets.'

There are also success stories concerning children. The members' committee from one centre wrote a personal letter to the headteacher of an adjoining school, complaining of abuse, which proved far more effective than numerous complaints from centre staff. Other groups have taken drama productions, about bullying, into schools or invited children to their centres. In one instance the result was a delegation from a group children to ask if they could do a similar play at the day centre – because they were being bullied as well.

Families

Families are often far from offering a safe environment to people with learning disabilities. Sexual offences are common. One study found that 13 per cent of all perpetrators were family members (Brown, Turk and Stein 1994).

Often there is an inclination for family members to ignore incidents because of the level of 'shame' that would follow a revelation of sexual offences against a person with learning disabilities. There are also more pragmatic reasons for covering up an incident, for example if parents have fought hard to put someone into residential care or a residential school and do not want to risk the arrangement ceasing.

People report assaults that are clearly deliberate, for example, one woman was constantly kicked by her father; another was locked in her room by a brother when her parents went out; another was tied up by a step-parent. But there is also a latent level of victimization from families stemming from inadequate support and services for people with behaviour problems.

> Linda [a 32-year-old woman with Down's Syndrome] related how her elderly uncle, the husband of her mother's sister, had been abusing her since she was twenty-four. This entailed touching her breasts and genitals and forcing sexual penetration... Linda was greatly concerned about her parents' reactions and also about the consequences, not so much for her uncle but for her aunt who was very ill...she was sure that what her uncle had been doing was wrong, even though he had told her, 'It's all right I'm not a blood relative.' At one point Linda wrote to her uncle telling him to stop or she would tell his wife. Her uncle stopped for a while but then became more threatening with his advances, 'holding' her down and stating he would tell everyone that she was the one responsible for this situation. Fearful of the consequences Linda felt powerless to stop the abuse until with great courage she disclosed to her doctor.
>
> Linda's parents were very shocked by the whole affair. They showed support to their daughter but scolded her for not telling them beforehand.
>
> Taylor 1993: 40

27

People with learning disabilities state the fear, common to many abusive family situations, that they do not want to report because they 'might get taken away by Social Services.'

The degree to which people suffer because they witness violence between family members has been recognised concerning children (Morgan and Zedner 1992: 21), and the same problem relates to people with learning disabilities. One woman made this very clear at a seminar on crime against people with learning disabilities,

> 'I saw my sister being hit by my brother-in-law. It made me feel afraid...unhappy'

Are families aware of the possible trauma caused to someone with learning disabilities by a heated argument that, to them, is just part of normal life? Unfortunately incidents are not always minor. Cases of young children witnessing horrible physical and sexual assaults on other family members are not unknown.

Financial offences are a particularly problematic aspect of victimization within families, because they are very difficult to prove and are often not seen by the perpetrators as violations of personal rights or the law. Social workers reported their concern to the police when the resident of a group home inherited a large sum of money and was immediately taken back into the family home by her parents. The house soon acquired a new conservatory, was completely refurbished, and the family bought a new car. Attempts to investigate were met with solicitor's letters, and approaches to the Court of Protection, which was administering the money, received no response. In circumstances such as this, families may believe, and sometimes be correct in assuming, that spending money to improve family circumstances is in the interests of the beneficiary. But did the beneficiary choose to spend the money in this way, with a full understanding of the other alternatives and of the amounts of money involved?

Colleagues at Work

The workplace is another setting for victimization, which often has long-lasting effects. A black man in his thirties relates how he had to give up his only job:

> 'I worked on a mushroom farm. I used to get a lot of abuse. People used to put dog-ends in my hair, spit at me and call me things like "wog" and "coon" – the managers knew all about it, but they did nothing.'

Another victim suffers discomfort, and problems when walking, from burns inflicted many years ago by workmates whose game of flicking lighted matches at him went wrong. The synthetic overall he was wearing caught fire.

She was raped in her own home, by the boyfriend of her cousin. He let himself into the woman's flat at a time he knew she would be alone. She was confused because her family persuaded her it hadn't happened, and she couldn't understand why no action was taken. The family put a lot of pressure on her to carry on as normal. She no longer feels safe living alone in her flat. The man who raped her still has access to her.

A Manchester man tells vividly how, whilst working for a taxi firm, he was wrongly accused of stealing a wallet. As a consequence, he was tied to an office chair and left for the night. He managed to escape, but was discovered and seriously assaulted, requiring hospitalization for a week. The person who stole the wallet eventually owned up, and although the police achieved a successful prosecution and compensation was paid, there was no possibility of the victim continuing the employment. Finding the confidence to work in a non-service setting remains difficult many years after the event.

Even training settings, within which a higher level of supervision might be expected, pose threats. A BBC news programme reported a string of incidents against a young man who was working within a mainstream Training and Enterprise Council scheme. People borrowed money without returning it, verbal insults were common, and he had bruises on his arms from being punched. As a result he left and is frightened to attempt a work placement again.

The workplace presents a specific problem concerning reporting. A number of people state that they did nothing about what was happening because of a fear of losing their job. The normal workplace dynamics of 'solidarity with workmates' and the power of immediate managers compound the disabilities.

The media

In 1991 a newspaper, the *Sun*, was successfully sued for describing a child with behaviour problems as the 'worst brat in Britain'. There are relatively few instances, such as this, in which the media directly victimizes people with learning disabilities. But secondary victimization is more common. The way that the media present reports can have helpful or very negative influences on the long-term outcomes of victimization.

Whilst the murder of a man in Bristol received insensitive treatment from a national newspaper, it had excellent coverage by the local press. The *Bristol Evening Post* offered a reward for information and presented the story factually without highlighting the victim's disability. The paper contributed to a feeling in the local community that, despite the disabilities faced by police investigators, everything possible was being done to catch the perpetrators. The murderer was eventually caught and convicted.

In great contrast, the reporting, by the *Daily Sport* (11 December 1992: 1,2), of the death of a woman, who was tied to a lavatory by nurses, appears thoroughly exploitative and would have had a wholly negative effect on family and friends.

29

The story appeared on the front page, and the headline, **TIED UP AND LEFT TO DIE**, was in two-inch letters. The statement was itself factually untrue, as it amounts to an incorrect allegation of an intention to kill. But of more concern, the headline was immediately beside a large photo of a 'page three' model – clad in nothing but chains. Only three short paragraphs of the story accompanied the headline.

The tabloids are not always so crass. A report in the *Daily Star* (22 February 1993: 11) about a man who was thrown in a river whilst fishing was sympathetic and factual, portraying appropriate images of victim, rescuer and perpetrators:

> After pulling him out, hero Andy said: 'How could people be so cruel? Simon's a bit slow, but he's a lovely chap.' Police are hunting the louts concerned.

An interesting example of changing press attitudes concerned the abduction of Jo Ramsden. Her story was taken up by the press after the *Independent*, drew a parallel between widespread coverage of the abduction of a 'classically attractive' Oxford student and the minimal attention paid to Jo Ramsden (5 May 1991: 5). Jo Ramsden's parents felt that, had more media attention been given to their daughter in the crucial first few weeks, it may have precipitated events leading to her discovery. The *Independent*, and other papers, then followed the story for over a year until the eventual trial of a suspect. Radio and television followed this lead.

One of the positive results was a very high level of awareness amongst people with learning disabilities of Jo's story, and of the dangers of abduction. A less happy outcome followed the acting out of the crime, on BBC *Crimewatch*, by another woman with Down's Syndrome. Her willingness to do this was itself a very brave act, but unfortunately her address was not kept confidential and she then suffered intrusive press harassment.

Media attitudes are slowly improving, but the importance of victims and their supporters dealing with reporters in a manner that does not lead to secondary victimization is very evident. The response of one reporter to complaints about insensitivity was very candid:

> 'Just tell us what to do. We don't mind, provided the intention is not to prevent a story appearing. Our insensitivity comes simply from the demands for speed which we face.'

This is helpful, but, in the light of the *Daily Sport*'s example, it seems that insensitivity may also stem from the ethos of the paper concerned.

30

The police

The subject of police victimization against minority groups is usually considered in relation to race, but people with learning disabilities occasionally suffer similar injustices. Of course, the stories of police abuse of power are more readily available than the countless examples of excellent practice. But, as with staff, any level of victimization by the police, however small, is an unacceptable breach of trust.

In Wales, a young man with learning disabilities, convicted of murdering a young girl, was later cleared because of the disclosure of police evidence suppressed at his trial. A senior officer and a forensic scientist were eventually charged with perverting the course of justice. Eleven police officers in Wales faced prosecution because of the wrongful conviction, for murder, of two men. Information about their propensity to confess to crimes they had not committed was not brought forward, and there was a suspicion of irregularities in police notebooks. The brothers also suffered at the hands of fellow prisoners because of a belief that they had committed sex crimes. A man who falsely confessed to armed robbery spent five months in prison:

> 'he was at the bottom of the prison pecking order. He became a 'boxing bag' for prison inmates, being beaten up and victimized frequently. He ended up having to do menial work for "prison bullies."' (Singhal 1992)

The facilities in one prison, in which prisoners with learning disabilities are held, is described in a recent report as resembling 'the impoverished environment of the backwards of the old asylums' (Liberty 1993:15).

Whilst some incidents make the headlines, there seems a worrying amount of low-level harassment by the police, although this may seem quite 'reasonable' from the perspective of the officers concerned. Tim Hart, of London People First, writes in *Disability Issues* (No.9 1992), 'Policemen always pick me up. Why is that when I haven't done anything wrong? They often think I have run away from home?' The police often use the Mental Health Act 1983 (s136) to pick up people 'for the protection of other persons...' but they commonly ignore the 'immediate' element in the Act and interpret group homes to be 'public places', probably incorrectly.

What is seen as helpful conduct by the police may be experienced as victimization by the people with learning disabilities. The dividing line is thin, but officers might ask themselves, 'What would be the position if this person did not obviously have learning disabilities?' In many circumstances, police actions might be seen as wrongful arrest, abduction, or false imprisonment by victims.

For information and advice about the rights of prisoners with physical disabilities and learning disabilities contact:
> Mikewatch
> c/o 6 Beulah View
> Leeds
> LS6 2LA

If a constable finds in a place to which the public have access a person who appears to him to be suffering from mental disorder and to be in immediate need of care or control, the constable may, if he thinks it necessary to do so in the interests of that person or for the protection of other persons, remove that person to a place of safety.

Mental Health Act 1983 s136 (1)

The stories that come to light, of course, tend to highlight negative incidents. So it is worth noting reports of exemplary pieces of police work in difficult circumstances. One case concerned a man with learning disabilities who was charged with rape of a woman resident:

> 'They were very sensitive in their interviewing, bending over backwards not to ask him leading questions, and very open to having a [lay] advocate there' (Citizen Advocate).

In a similar example staff conclude, 'The police were amazing – very sensitive – more like social workers than us!'

Police officers agree that much regrettable interaction with people with learning disabilities stems from the problem of recognizing that an individual has an intellectual disability. Officers also express the concern that they may cause offence to other members of the public if they suggest that, for example, someone with cerebral palsy or a hearing impairment, has learning disabilities. (The officer who asked a London man, 'Are you a nutter?' obviously did not share these reservations!) Recognition, without causing unnecessary offence, could be greatly improved through using a simple staged process:

1. **observation**
2. **general questions** that are not directly related to intellectual disability
3. **specific questions** that relate to disability.

The suggested format (following page) builds on work from Australia (Johnson, Andrew and Topp 1988: Appendix 2) the National Autistic Society, and has been developed with the help of UK self-advocacy groups, professionals and police. The information can be presented as a handout, wallchart, or prompt card.

The general police officer is unlikely to deal with victims with learning disabilities on more than a handful of occasions throughout a career. There can be no pretence that police training could, or should, embrace a substantial input about learning disabilities. But a complete absence of awareness training is not excusable – people with learning disabilities form 3 per cent of the population an officer is supposed to serve.

At the police training school in Hendon, cadets used to work with people with intellectual and mental health disabilities over a period of six weeks; now one afternoon at a day centre is rare and cadets can leave with an ill-formed perspective. Transport police, who will have a higher than average exposure to people with learning disabilities and mental health problems, often have no specific training.

One day I went to the hairdressers and asked for 50p to get home on the bus because I had lost my money. The hairdresser phoned the police and they came and they said to me, 'Where are you going?'. I said, 'Can you take me to Antrim Forum?' and they said, 'Jump into the car and we'll take you there.' After a few minutes I said, 'You're going the wrong way' and they said, 'We're taking you to the mental hospital.'

There were two policemen in the back with me...I was very frightened and didn't know what to do. I had nightmares about it afterwards. What the police should have done was contact Social Services to see who I was; that was if they felt they couldn't ask me.

I did nothing wrong just asking for 50p. The hairdresser did apologise to me afterwards but the police didn't.

James Hatten, letter to Opengate, Summer 1993

if an officer has any suspicion, or is told in good faith, that a person of any age may be...mentally handicapped, or mentally incapable of understanding the significance of questions put to him or his replies, then that person shall be treated as a...mentally handicapped person for the purpose of this code.

Police and Criminal Evidence Act
Code of Practice, para 1.4

There is no easy way to know if people have

Learning Disabilities
(Mental Handicap, Learning Difficulties)

They **may** have difficulty

> **speaking**
>
> **moving**
>
> **understanding**
>
> **reading and writing**
>
> **telling the time**
>
> remembering their **date of birth, age, address, telephone number**
>
> knowing the **day of the week, where they are, and who you are.**

They **may**

> also have **physical disabilities, visual or hearing impairments**
> (but most people with physical disabilities do **not** have learning disabilities)
>
> appear **very eager to please** or **repeat what you say.**

Ask   **where they live.** Do they live in a group home, hostel, hospital or,
          as an adult, still live with parents?

> **where they work.** Do they attend a special work scheme?
>
> **where they went to school.** Was it a special school?

Ask if they

> carry **special identification**
>
> have a **social worker** or **key worker**
>
> go to a **Day Centre** ('ATC', 'RAC', 'SEC')
>
> get a **disabled living allowance**
>
> are a member of **People First, Mencap, a Gateway club**

Ask

> 'Do people say you have **learning disabilities** or are **mentally handicapped?**'

If the **pattern** of answers suggests that a person has a learning disability,
and you want more help, contact

_____

or the duty social worker

Suspects with learning disabilities must have an **appropriate adult** present when questioned (PACE).
Victims and witnesses should have support from an independent person.

Victimization and inappropriate actions from the police usually stem from two problems: failure to *recognize* that a victim or suspect has learning disabilities, and an absence of *knowledge about sources of support nationally, within and outside the police*.

Failures of police in their duty are often seen by people with learning disabilities as a form of victimization. There are frequent stories of the police not responding to reports by victims with learning disabilities. Another common complaint is that, during an initial interview, officers give an impression that the victim is in the wrong. In one example, the officer clearly sympathized with the alleged perpetrator, and delivered a lecture stating as much, emphasizing the 'good name' of the institution concerned and of the alleged perpetrator. This was backed up with the *perpetrator's* view of a specific law – a view which was an incorrect interpretation. The officer admitted later that he had no detailed knowledge of the statute he had quoted to the victim.

Victims often state feelings to the effect that, after a police interview, 'It made me feel as though I was the criminal.' What hope is there then for a productive interview in the future? How, with such an approach, would officers find out if an initial complaint was simply the tip of an iceberg? **All officers investigating complaints by vulnerable victims should follow the basic precept that initially any story, however improbable, should be accepted at face value, without any intimation of disbelief or that the matter is too minor for police involvement. If a complaint turns out to be improper this should be explained with great care, after a full investigation.**

The problem is to isolate examples of poor police practice which are clearly based on improper assumptions about the victim or a prejudice about learning disabilities. One housing trust had made a number of complaints to police, concerning damage and threatening behaviour around a particular house, which were ignored. They were later told by a community officer just to use the address of the home when reporting, because using the name, or anything that would indicate that the house was a group home, would lead to the report ending up in the bin.

One man was, on separate occasions, gored by a bull and injured by a hit-and-run driver. In both instances police were informed but did not go to interview him because they believed that he could not tell them what happened. Fortunately the victim's sister was a police officer in another force, so appropriate action was subsequently taken. (Case stories in a form suitable for police training are included in Appendix One.)

A decision not to pursue an inquiry or prosecution, on the grounds that a victim has learning disabilities should, as a matter of policy, not be taken by individual, 'front-line' police officers.

I have very often turned around in the street, and sniggered when I've seen handicapped people go by. But now I was to be head to head with about twenty of them... At first I began to speak to her like a small child, and [she] just let me watch her do it all. But as I watched the other staff with the others, I realised that these people were adults, they were double my own age, and I was treating them like babies. This is where my mind clicked...The moral was, never to judge a book by its cover...There were many that couldn't communicate with you by speech, but I learnt to somehow make contact with them, just by eye contact, facial expressions and hand and body movements.

Their slow learning disabilities mixed with physical impairments didn't mean that you should pretend you understood them, when talking...they respect you more if you're straight with them. I learned to treat them as normal people. It took me a long time to get to know the clients here however. All the times the clients play you up are worth it when a client who can't walk or talk hugs you.

Metropolitan Police Cadets,
reporting on day centre placements

34

The justice system

The justice system provides the main example of abuses of power, which are not contrary to law, but which are seen by people with learning disabilities as clear victimization. Is this ethos acceptable, and if not, what measures can be taken to ensure redress for victims?

Until very recently, the main abuse of power stemmed from the way in which 'the system', quite lawfully, punished people who could not reasonably have been held responsible for their actions. Diversionary schemes, directing such offenders away from punitive responses, are now starting to operate more effectively. But people with learning disabilities still end up in prison simply because the court does not recognize that they have a disability.

In one case the only support an offender received was a hand written letter from a social worker. The judge found this difficult to read and commented, 'Learning disabilities – does that mean he had difficulty at school?' A prison sentence was immediately imposed, without further consideration.

Full Pre-Sentence Reports, which can include a psychiatric assessment, are not available to magistrates unless they are considering a custodial sentence. Information such as a defendant's previous attendance at a special school might be ignored, and petty offenders are punished without any recognition of their disability. Some offences do not qualify for legal aid, so a defendant with learning disabilities might appear in court completely unrepresented. Without representation or help, a person with learning disabilities may be fined a large amount for not having a TV licence for a TV he or she did not own. He or she may later brought back as a fine defaulter, and eventually imprisoned (in this case without a pre-sentence report) for non-payment. In the event of another minor offence, the individual has a record showing a period in prison which increases the subsequent sentence. No court official has the stated duty to recognise and divert offenders with intellectual disabilities. **Specific responsibility should be given to the clerk in magistrates' courts, to identify petty offenders with learning disabilities, to ensure that magistrates seek a proper assessment, and to propose appropriate diversionary measures.**

Without unprejudiced and enlightened attitudes from judges, there seems little hope for reducing victimization within the justice system. What are the precedents set by the report of a case in which a manager of a day centre had allegedly grabbed the man by the lapels, shaken him against a wall and slapped him around the face with both hands? The judge, when directing a jury to return a 'not guilty' verdict on a point of law, reportedly said,

> 'It was not a serious act of violence.'

Mr P had meningitis as a child, which left him brain-damaged... he was taken to court for non-payment of council tax worth £250 and was ordered to pay £10 per week. He made two payments but forgot to make any more. In May 1993, he was ordered to attend a second hearing. It is not clear how he got to court. He could not have read a summons, cannot use public transport unaided, and could not walk, owing to the recent removal of a cancerous growth from his foot. His sister believes that he was taken by a warrant officer... Mr P had no legal representation in court (there is no legal aid for council tax defaulters). He was found guilty and sentenced to 28 days' imprisonment. After six days he was released on bail pending judicial review (council tax defaulters have no right of appeal), and the High Court eventually overturned the sentence, ruling that it was 'unreasonable'.

Independent, Sunday Review, 12 June 1994: 11

and then 'likened the incident to a parent smacking a child, and later regretting the action.' The victim was 48 years old (*Western Telegraph* (Dyfed) 27 March 1991). A remarkable precedent was set in the Scottish courts when a Sheriff maintained that throwing cold water on patients and striking them were reasonable control and restraint methods under the Mental Health Act (See Ashton and Ward 1992: 133).

Sentencing can also appear erratic and unjust. An employee who had been promoted to a social worker with people with learning disabilities from odd-job man, and had then sexually assaulted a woman client, only received a sentence of three years' probation. The Judge rationalized this by saying,

> 'I am taking an exceptionally lenient course with you. I am doing it because I think you were driven beyond endurance... I don't understand how anyone can go from maintenance worker one day to a social worker the next in a house like this dealing with difficult young people.' (*The Guardian* August 31 1991: 5).

Of course judges also relate the circumstances of vulnerability in other, more positive, ways. A residential manager, who raped a resident, was told by the judge that the sentence was severe because he specifically took account of the 'not guilty' plea which had forced the victim through the ordeal of a court appearance.

Defence lawyers have a particular duty to their clients, but sometimes their behaviour when dealing with prosecution witnesses with learning disabilities seems to have more to do with abuse of power than eliciting the truth. What, in terms of evidence, did the defence barrister hope to achieve by asking a victim of a sexual assault, 'You wet the bed every night and you think that someone would want to sleep with you'? When one lawyer asked a victim-witness to move to the centre of the court, was this really because he could not hear her replies, or because this put her close to her alleged assailant – a proximity she found unnerving?

From regularly observing the same lawyers' behaviour towards witnesses who have obvious vulnerabilities, the following approaches seem to be quite common.

> repeating the same question many times
>
> leaving long silences
>
> pretending not to hear answers
>
> demonstrations of temper tantrums such as throwing papers on the desk
>
> a sudden contrast between very gentle and then very aggressive questioning
>
> congratulating witnesses on 'cleverness'
>
> asking a string of irrelevant questions to which the answer is, 'yes', and then one crucial question requiring 'no'.

Judge's comments echo 'silly' remarks

Judge Sir Harold Cassell QC, refused to jail an ex-policeman for indecently assaulting his 12-year-old mentally retarded stepdaughter.

He said the man was driven to assault the girl because his wife's pregnancy had dimmed her sexual appetite, causing 'considerable problems for a healthy young husband'.

Judge Cassell was strongly rebuked by Lord Mackay, the Lord Chancellor, and retired early on medical grounds.

Guardian, June 10 1993: 3

36

In one instance an obviously distressed woman disclosed the defendant's previous convictions, in her answer to a defending lawyer's question. The lawyer immediately asked for a re-trial, stating that he had earlier warned the woman not to mention the previous conviction. Yet the question he asked could only be answered truthfully by disclosure of the conviction. The victim-witness ran from the court in tears.

It is often difficult to assess whether or not abuse from lawyers is intentional, or just indicative of the narrowmindness and prejudice of the individual. One lawyer told a court,

> 'He's a comical character. He stutters. He's the sort of person children would have made fun of in the playground. He's inadequate. He's slightly simple. He's easy prey for those intent on a game or schoolboy pranks. He's like a child – very naive. He's not a sophisticated man. He could easily be teased by those who are younger than him. This man has little to offer the world.'

This particular character assassination was carried out by the lawyer *acting on behalf* of a man with learning disabilities. In a similar example, the solicitor stated, of a man who had just moved into a community setting, 'When he was in hospital, he never left the grounds, so he had no need for clothes'. Whilst individually these incidents may seem trivial, the cumulative effect is to foster negative attitudes and relegate people with learning disabilities to a second-class position in the justice system.

The Crown Prosecution Service (CPS) is also part of the overall picture. Reports that prosecutions have been dropped because the CPS considers that a witness with learning disabilities cannot give credible evidence, are quite common. Usually this decision is made without meeting the victim – a prejudice that *all* people with learning disabilities are incapable of relating events clearly.

Inappropriate practice within the justice system is important as it has a 'kick-back' effect which increases the possibility of criminal victimization. Because the present ethos of courts leads to few convictions, the CPS drop cases on the grounds of a low 'likelihood of conviction'. Consequently the police have an excuse for not referring cases to the CPS, and the message to perpetrators is that there is nothing to be feared from victimizing people with learning disabilities.

Neo-nazi victimization

As yet there seems to be no evidence, in the UK, of the type of motivation for victimization presently found in Germany: Nazi-style attacks aimed at 'cleansing' the community of people with disabilities.

> *A male victim of a sexual assault related how the defending barrister pretended not to hear him so frequently that the judge eventually asked, 'Isn't it obvious what he said?' The victim points out that the stenographer had no difficulty hearing. When he apologized for not understanding something and said that he sometimes had trouble with long words, the barrister then went on to congratulate him when he used long words, at one point turning to the jury and saying,*
>> *'Homophobic – isn't that a long word ladies and gentlemen?'*

One study in Germany, by Detlev Jahnert, relates how it is quite common for disabled people to be told by passers by that they 'should have been gassed' or 'have no place in a clean Germany' (Tomforde 1994:9). There are reports of attacks on special schools. In Siegen two skinheads face trial for kicking to death a man who was almost blind.

Is there no victimization of this nature in the UK or is it possible that there is, as yet, no recognition of Nazi-style motivation? An official document from the British National Party talks of disabled people as 'physical degenerates who are a burden on the state medical system'. What about the persecution of people in group homes by neighbours who do not want them in the neighbourhood? To what degree can broken windows and damage to staff cars be equated with the German situation?

Organizational victimization

The victimization so far discussed embodies direct perpetrator–victim relationships. But there is also victimization by organizations where direct links between perpetrator and victim are not clear, yet laws are broken and people with learning disabilities suffer as a result. Users of social or health services may be particularly at risk, and the outcomes are sometimes far from minor.

In one institution a woman of 65 died because of a breakdown of communications between medical staff. Hospital doctors failed to recognize a fractured skull and the woman was returned to her long-stay hospital where the seriousness of her condition was not realized. The injury resulted from being pushed over by another patient. The reported outcome, following an inquest, was not a better personal safety policy, but the setting up of a working group to consider 'the diagnoses and management of handicapped people with head injuries'.

In another example a young man died after a 'scuffle' following an argument with another resident at his home triggered heart failure related to a rare, and undiagnosed, heart condition. Individual staff cannot be blamed directly, yet should the ethos of a person's home be unsafe to the degree that unwelcome assaults can happen? A care ethos that considered personal safety to be pre-eminent might have prevented both these deaths.

Organizational victimization is more often experienced as an on-going pattern of minor events than a single incident. The parents of a young woman with learning disabilities committed suicide, killing their daughter as well, by connecting a pipe from the exhaust of their car to the interior. This followed twenty years of dissatisfaction with the services they had received.

> *One problem I have encountered when people with learning disabilities are moving into a house is, the resistance by neighbours to accept them... Windows have been broken, break-ins have occurred, general nuisance and verbal abuse... Once when preparing a house for people to move in a break-in occurred and paint was splashed over newly papered walls. I abandoned this move as the people would not stand a chance if they moved in.*

Alex Fish, ATC Manager, Falkirk

38

The parents left a note stating that, 'we went on as long as we could, but doctors and social workers... couldn't care less... and we finally have given in'. At the inquest there was evidence of instances of apparent bad practice. These included an admission that the family's social worker did not know if he was the worker for the whole family or just for the woman with learning disabilities. The social services' defence to the suggestion of a failure of duty to care, at the inquest, was that it only had the 'power' to provide services, not a 'duty'.

The inquest verdict in this case could not include 'failure of duty to care' because the proximate cause of death was clearly the actions of the parents. However, in another case, where a 20-year-old man with epilepsy and cerebral palsy choked eating a sandwich whilst left unattended by care assistants, 'death by natural causes brought about by lack of care' was recorded (Inquest into the death of Anthony Arkwright, St Helens, H.M. Coroner G.H.H. Glasgow, 1993).

It might be difficult to argue that maladministration concerning Social Securities benefits can be considered 'victimization', but from the complainant's perspective outcomes are not dissimilar to those of common theft. The Department of Social Security had to be taken to the High Court concerning a clothing grant for 'a man who spent 29 years in hospital wearing only pyjamas'. He had been moved into accommodation provided by a housing association and the benefits office maintained that grants were only available if people moved into 'the community' and that sheltered housing was not 'the community'.

Within all types of service organization there remains a sad lack of regard for the rights of people with learning disabilities. What other explanation can be given to the report that the Department of Social Security told a parent to lock her daughter up at night to cut costs?

It is arguable that anyone who suggests (i.e. 'counsels') locking up an individual unlawfully would be guilty of complicity if the advice was followed. The law of complicity should be carefully considered by anyone who gives advice in a professional capacity.

MUM TOLD TO LOCK UP HER DOWNS DAUGHTER

A mentally handicapped teenager has had her state benefit cut after an official suggested she could be locked up at night to reduce her need for care and supervision...The DSS adjudication officer's report [states] '...Ellen does not show any dangerous tendencies, and the bedroom door could be locked to prevent her from wandering. Therefore, I do not consider that watching over her is required at night'...

In a similar case three years ago, [concerning] a Scottish woman with severe epilepsy...the Social Security Commissioners ruled the decision had been unreasonable. 'To lock the house door...would be to impose a form of house arrest; more importantly it could have dangerous consequences in the event of fire.'

The Observer, 19 December 1993: 2

Any person who...counsels...the commission of any indictable offence...is liable to be tried and punished as a principal offender...it is not necessary to show that the counselling was a substantial cause of the commission of the offence...

Halsbury's Laws Vol 11 (1) para 43

39

A very specific example of victimization experienced by service users concerns their right to see personal files. Excuses such as, 'They have been destroyed' or, 'They are distributed around many different agencies' are often reported. As a matter of good practice, it is also arguable that notes on adults with learning disabilities should now be made in simple English so that clients have the possibility of understanding them. The Access to Health Records Act 1990 makes it clear that professionals must explain anything that is not understood.

Occasionally Health and Safety Regulations have been used to pursue a case of neglect against an organization. A school was fined following the drowning of a boy with epilepsy, on the basis that it had failed to assess properly the risks associated with swimming and the boy's epilepsy. The boy had been dead in the school's lake for more than an hour before he was missed.

Outside service organizations, a significant, yet less direct, example of organizational victimization concerns employment. Under the Disabled Persons (Employment) Acts 1944 and 1958 every employer outside the public sector, employing more than 20 people, must ensure that 3% of its employees are registered disabled. Employers must keep records and produce them for inspection. A permit must be obtained to employ non-disabled people, if the quota has not been met. Since 1944 there have only been 10 prosecutions, the last in 1975, with fines averaging £62. Only 20,000 permits are issued each year. Amongst other government agencies, the Department of Health and the Home Office fail to meet these requirements. It is unsurprising that the estimated number of people with learning disabilities who have employment is only 5% nationally. In Germany a similar scheme is enforced rigorously.

Discrimination within transport organizations against people with learning disabilities is also a concern. A driver who did not permit a person with learning disabilities to enter a bus would almost certainly be breaking transport regulations, but more subtle forms of abuse (complaining that an individual is too slow or unintelligible, for example) are not a basis for formal action against the perpetrators. Sadly if people have bad experiences with bus drivers they are unlikely to report to them any offences committed against them by fellow passengers.

There are, course, reports of extreme helpfulness from bus drivers. In one case abusive children were removed from a bus. In another case the driver took the opportunity to publicly deliver a lesson to a group of young boys about human values and respect for human rights.

The absence of specific anti-discrimination legislation in the UK leads to circumstances which would constitute offences against disabled people if they happened in other countries.

...any authority keeping records containing personal information which is accessible personal information...shall have such obligations as regards access to, and the accuracy of, that information...

'Personal information' means information which relates to a living individual who can be identified from that information (or from that and other information in the possession of the authority keeping the record).

Access to Personal Files Act 1987, 1 (1); 2 (2)

The Access to Personal Files (Social Services) Regulations 1989 gives individuals the right to see their manually held Social Services file. The authority is obliged to tell an individual whether they hold information concerning that person, and to provide access to that information.

The Access to Health Records Act 1990 provides that people can see and copy any information which has been manually recorded on their health records. This includes information 'relating to the physical or mental health of an individual' or 'has been made by or on behalf of a health professional in connection with the care of that individual'

Ashton and Ward 1992: 142– 6

> The driver didn't let me on the bus and she told me to get on the one behind. I asked her why and she said, 'Because I don't like you.' I said, 'No, I've got a right to get on.' She started cursing me, but before I got off she said sorry. I said, 'I should think so.'

> This man took his trousers down when I was on top in the bus. He was horrible. I was very afraid. I didn't tell the driver because he wasn't very friendly. I told my mum and we went to the bus station but they said it was too late to do anything.

Efforts to introduce a Civil Rights (Disabled Persons) Bill in 1994 were frustrated because the British government felt that anti-discrimination legislation was not necessary, and because of fears about the cost. As a consequence restaurants, cinemas, leisure and sports facilities can still legally say 'No disabled people admitted.' The UK government upholds their view despite the precedent of the Americans with Disabilities Act, and similar legislation in China, a country that British politicians frequently condemn for its poor human rights record.

But organizational victimization can be changed , even within organizations that are usually considered beyond reproach. In 1993 London People First won a landmark victory over the Charities Commission. The Commission had previously refused People First's request for charitable status on the grounds that the trustees were legally incapable of exercising adequate judgement. It is those who are on the receiving end of unfair treatment who are the strongest force for change.

3

CHAPTER

Prevention

Prevention strategies

Learning about prevention is best approached through the personal experiences of people with learning disabilities. Many people have a high awareness of crime from fictional TV programmes and series such as *Crimewatch*. Using cuttings from newspapers is another excellent way of opening a discussion, and the examples from Chapters One and Two would provide more specific material. Ideas for teaching self-protection skills are discussed by Haseltine and Miltenberger (1990), and a group of people with learning disabilities has produced the *Walsall Women's Group Safety Video – No means No* (WWG 1994). A publication from NAPSAC *It could Never Happen Here!* deals more practically with the prevention and treatment of sexual abuse of adults with learning disabilities in residential settings (1993).

Day centres often invite crime prevention officers to give presentations. Sometimes centres run more elaborate personal safety classes. Training on sexuality and assertiveness skills is increasing. In a few instances people attend self-defence classes. Women's safety, particularly concerning transport, can be viewed separately (see Korn 1992). It is also valuable to discuss potentially unsafe situations that are more relevant to men, such as football matches and fights in pubs. Some service providers have formed good links with local police, service users get to know individual officers well, and prevention advice is on-going.

Avoiding advertising vulnerability is a more specific aspect of prevention. Often the appearance of buildings and the way staff interact with service users in public can suggest that people may be vulnerable. Burglary, opportunist theft and confidence tricks may all result from a criminal's assessment of the occupants of a house or the capabilities of individuals.

Incidents concerning friends provide a good basis for discussing avoidance of victimization. Following the murder of a Bristol man, friends discussed personal safety on the basis of conjecture about the actual circumstances of his death. They concluded:

- Don't stand at bus stops late at night unless you know a bus is due.

- Remember, you can use a bus if you have no money, just tell the driver your name and address.

- Tell someone where you are going and when you expect to be back.

- Don't dress in expensive clothes for walking in the street. Don't show off expensive watches, wallets, or anything people might want to steal.

- If people start bothering you, try not to look scared. Get help quickly by going into a shop or public building.

What are the messages, (given to potential abusers), about the vulnerability of people with learning disabilities, by staff actions such as those mentioned in this letter in the *Guardian*?

> '...one person has no road sense and when he is out walking he wears a Mothercare Junior Lead Rein to ensure his safety' (Letter from a residential manager, 27 July 1993, p19).

Similarly, is it really necessary for a newspaper to publish a *map* of the places from which a number of people with learning disabilities have been abducted? What more help could other potential abductors wish for? Even in court, there seems a lack of awareness about advertising vulnerability. Whilst detailed evidence about exploitation may be unavoidable, was there really any need for one judge to comment, concerning a woman with learning disabilities, '...the voice of a three-year-old from the lips of an attractive 22-year-old woman'?

Police presence is increasingly constrained by financial considerations, but there are a few innovative ideas worth exploring. Simple measures can often be effective and reassuring. Individuals being able to quote the names of police officers, or carrying cards with the name and photo of the Community Police Officer which can be shown to abusers, can be useful. One women recalls,

> 'These boys came up to me and started pulling my hair and shouting at me. I said, "I'll tell my friend Dave Jones about you. He's a policeman. He'll soon sort you out." They went away then.'

The occasional appearance of uniformed officers in the vicinity of day centres and residential homes, can remind potential offenders that their actions may not go unreported. Another women explains,

> 'I had a lot of trouble with school kids. We told the police and next day, when I was waiting at a bus stop, this police car pulled up and the officer said to me, "Hello. Are these the kids that are bothering you? Don't worry, I've had a good look at them." There's been no more trouble.'

People with learning disabilities experience much victimization on buses. In London, the police are now given bus passes by the operators, with the effect that they now have a high level of free policing of their buses.

The **protective use of transport**, especially cars, is widely acknowledged by adults who would otherwise consider themselves to be very vulnerable walking on the streets, for example women and older people. But very few people with learning disabilities drive. Greater consideration should be given to the mobility needs of people who are not necessarily physically disabled, but whose mobility is impaired because of the threats posed by criminality within their community.

Vulnerability can be advertised by:

things that suggest the physical weakness of residents

- disability logos
- signs such as 'Ambulances Only'
- hand rails
- conspicuous ramps
- conspicuous ambulances

the 'institutional look' of a building

- social/health service or local authority notices
- unaesthetic placing of dustbins
- gardens without any 'human touches'
- obvious staff car parks (which can also advertise when there is no, or only one, staff member on site)
- regularity such as 'lights out' at the same time each night

the way staff interact with service users in public

- making people walk in 'crocodile' lines
- unnecessary shouted warnings about traffic or behaviour
- over-protective care concerning the use of money
- patronizing or 'baby talk'

Personal safety programmes for people with learning disabilities could usefully embrace the protective use of transport. Topics can include

- how to minimize the time waiting at bus stops and train stations

- how to plan journeys for safety, and what to do when things go wrong

- what to do if you have no money (it is possible to use most forms of public transport by giving a name and address)

- when and how to make an 'emergency' decision to use a taxi.

Functionally, street crime often imposes a mobility impairment on people with learning disabilities. **State mobility benefits, should be reviewed to include the 'protective use' of taxis and special transport schemes by people who may be vulnerable because of intellectual disabilities**.

Helpless victims?

Many people with learning disabilities are very far from being helpless victims. One man foiled an attempted burglary by pushing the intruder off a window sill, breaking his arm in the process. A very quiet woman reported,

> 'I was on the bus and some school children were making fun of me. They were calling me mental, and making funny faces. I got off the bus and they were chucking paper at me. I hit them with the umbrella'

Whilst stories like this make good reading, it is easy to see how things could go wrong when people stand up for themselves – they might easily be seen as the perpetrator. Preparation is one answer. A woman who walked into her flat to 'find a guy lifting my video equipment' scared him away by screaming and setting off her personal alarm.

Less problematic are simple **avoidance strategies** such as crossing over the road if a situation looks dangerous. Unfortunately, group discussions often lead to unfortunate stereotyping, for example that all black youths are dangerous. The best response is to emphasize the avoidance strategies rather than an analysis of what constitutes a threatening situation – 'If **you** feel threatened, avoid the problem. Never mind what other people might do.'

Defusing a threatening situation by a quick comment seems one of the most effective approaches. One man averted a threat of robbery by drunken youths simply by saying, 'You do, and I'll set my dog on you.' A woman tells how she was waiting at a bus stop and a man in a car pulled up and said,

> 'Hello duck. You look OK. Get in and come home for coffee.' Her reply was simple and effective, 'Not bloody likely. I don't fancy you. I'm not that hard up.'

A man, recently appointed to do clerical work at a university, who was constantly accosted by aggressive beggars, reported that he now has no problems because,

> 'I told them to go and get a job, like me.'

It is perhaps less important what is said and more important that a quick, confident and probably unexpected retort is given. If nothing else, for a perpetrator who thinks that he or she is dealing with a helpless individual, the surprise element may be enough to discourage further actions.

> *I was walking home, helping someone who could not walk. These yobs – they were pushing a barrow – attacked me. I was pushed up an alley. They smashed my glasses and hit me in the face. I ended up in hospital with stitches... But the police got them. I sat on one of them until the people from the shops called the police. They took photos of me, and took the blood off the man's shoes. I didn't have to go to court.*

> *We had a lot of trouble on the bus. These boys would wind down the window after we had closed it – every time. So one day we got in and wound it down. They wound it up. But that was fine because it was boiling hot and we wanted it open – any fool could see that. And we told them so.*

45

Learning effective comments, and discussing those that may not work or make things worse, is a very simple skill to practice in personal safety groups.

People with learning disabilities are also clearly a part of crime prevention for the whole community, not least because they are often at home when many people are at work. One woman who discovered burglars next door, because her dog was barking, alerted the police who made an quick arrest. When asked how she managed to achieve such a quick response from the police, she replied, 'I just told them to shift their arses and get here quick.' Stories of handing in lost property to police stations are common, in one case resulting in a large reward. Crime prevention can also happen at work. An employee at a DIY store pointed out a man who looked suspicious to the manager, and sure enough the man did steal something. The employee says he took note of the offender because,

> 'He looked like a Gizmo gangster – just like those criminals on *Crimewatch*. So I kept an eye on him.'

Self-advocacy groups can sometimes have more effect than formal attempts to achieve crime prevention measures. Ken Simons reports a case when a day centre had been burgled four times, and the manager had met with no success at getting the authority to install an alarm. The centre committee took up the fight and wrote to councillors, with the result: 'The councillors were moved enough to come and talk to the users and within a couple of days someone was sent down from County Hall to see what system was needed.' (Simons 1992: 54). In another example, British Telecom were pursued to waive the deposit for a person, who had no previous record of payment, because he needed a phone to report on-going victimization by children. He also used his CB radio to get help.

Basic crime prevention strategies should include:

> **education based on existing awareness and life-experiences**
>
> **the protective use of transport**
>
> **learning avoidance strategies**
>
> **encouraging a visible police presence amongst people with learning disabilities**
>
> **an avoidance of 'advertising vulnerability'**
>
> **a recognition that people with learning disabilities can be part of general crime prevention in the community.**

A group of handicapped people say they are being driven to despair by cruel taunts of children... Now members of Croydon's People First plan to fight back by taking the battle for fair treatment into schools. They want to explain that while they might be a bit slow, they are just the same as anyone else. 'And just as able to feel hurt by being called names... At first I didn't know what to do, but then I decided to go down to Chipstead Valley primary School. After that I never had any trouble. In fact, we became good friends.'

Reported by Hilary Brook

Preventing victimization by peers

Staff sometimes express a view about victimization between people with learning disabilities along the lines that,

> 'They are all as bad as one another, so they just have to put up with it.'

Even if it were true that everyone in a particular service setting constantly offended, the solution in 'ordinary life' is not to let this happen.

In one day centre a man was observed walking round in circles and regularly clipping a woman behind the ear. When challenged, the manager said,

> 'Oh, they always do that.'

What did the manager mean by 'they', when there is a clear victim–victimizer relationship? More importantly, the messages this situation sends to those concerned are

- (to the perpetrator) this behaviour is OK – you could walk into a cafe and do this

- (to the victim) you must put up with being assaulted because you have learning disabilities. If this happens to you in a cafe ignore it. Don't bother telling anyone because they won't do anything.

Managers and staff also argue 'We must take risks, if we are to integrate people with challenging behaviour into the community.' It is, of course, commendable for staff to hold this opinion about risks to themselves. But should staff have the power to take risks with perpetrators which create a threat to other people with learning disabilities? It is uncomfortable logic to suppose that people with learning disabilities are likely to have a greater tolerance of victimization just because the perpetrator also has learning disabilities. Are staff who express this view sometimes trying to prove something about their own professional expertise at the expense of service users?

Much peer victimization stems from habits learned in long-stay hospitals. Not only have some people learned offending behaviour, many have been conditioned to tolerate it. **When people move into community settings, part of their education should include an awareness of what crime is and of the possibilities of getting a criminal record for behaviour that may have been 'accepted' as normal in hospital.**

Reports of sexual offences between people with learning disabilities often embrace three basic factors:

a known history of the perpetrator's sexual promiscuity:
'This man was married but known to womanize with centre clients and had sexual relationships with at least four others.'

known power relationships:
'The victim was sexually abused by another brighter member of the training centre.'

a known history of previous victimization:
'her mother indicated that she had aborted several pregnancies for her daughter...Rumours indicate that the victim has been abused before.'

This framework may help staff to identify unsafe situations.

If service managers have any doubts about the need to prevent victimization between service users, they might note that civil claims against social and health authorities are not unknown. Victimization including biting and scratching and attempted sexual assault has constituted the basis for claims of failing to properly supervise perpetrators and to ensure the victim's safety. Where there has been no police involvement, and consequently the chance to claim from the Criminal Injuries Compensation Board has been denied, a damages claim will include the sum that might otherwiwe have been forthcoming from the Board. More broadly, a precedent has been set by a case against a Scottish school, brought by a woman who claims that her exam results, and therefore career, were affected because of bullying (Renton 1993: 11).

Managers should introduce a 'safety first' policy in all service settings. If this means one-to-one staffing to prevent victimization, this is probably cheaper for society in the long run than resorting to secure units and dealing with the trauma or resultant challenging behaviour of victims.

Staff and volunteers

Whilst most people with learning disabilities continue to spend a large part of their lives in constant contact with staff, staff will remain a key element in prevention. Ensuring that staff do not have a record of offending is becoming an increasing concern. Of equal importance is the need for induction programmes and training that create a thorough awareness of the law in relation to service settings. At present knowledge of the law is seen as the domain of senior managers, yet it is front-line staff who are more likely to have the opportunity (knowingly or unknowingly) to victimize, and who have direct influence concerning minor victimization by others.

At present there is no requirement for police checks on workers employed to work with adults with learning disabilities, as there are concerning those working with children (except in Northern Ireland), though checks are required of managers or owners of care homes (see Jones 1993: 164). The police are rarely willing to make checks that are not mandatory, but it is worth noting that local arrangements are possible.

The Department of Health argues that legislation concerning police checks on general staff is not necessary, and that the employer should ask for references and ensure that they are followed up (Ferriman 1992: 5). (This comment was made following the murder of a disabled woman by someone who was employed on the basis of a false reference, which had been followed up.) Relying on references not only assumes that the referees and the people who are followed-up are always trustworthy, but also that referees know about all relevant convictions. They may not have this knowledge because of the absence of police checks previously.

If police checks are considered desirable, service providers might consider introducing a policy that all staff are employed generically, i.e. on the basis that any employee might be called upon to work with children and therefore will be checked.

Staff generally know that violence should be avoided and that there is a duty to care. But they often are not aware that many of their daily actions, and those of others, might constitute offences. Staff induction and training should include an awareness of aspects of criminal law in relation to their jobs, listed on the following pages. (These are exemplified further in Chapters 1 and 2.)

Appropriate induction can increase staff and volunteer awareness of offences they might unknowingly commit, and of actions by others that should be treated as offences.

Staff can be advised that if they feel they cannot do their job without the possibility of committing offences, or other people committing offences, this should be communicated directly to senior management in writing.

Trade unions might usefully inform their members about the law in relation to their job. They should also negotiate with managers to ensure that employees are not forced into circumstances where they, or anyone else, might commit offences.

49

Any deprivation of liberty, without consent, could be 'false imprisonment', if not imposed under the Mental Health Act or for safety reasons in an emergency.

Any form of touching, without consent, might be a common assault unless done for safety reasons in an emergency. Assault can result from an act that is intentional or *reckless*.

Aggressive shouting or gestures, which may cause a person to fear violence, outside a 'dwelling' may be an offence against the Public Order Act 1986. Staff should assume that public areas such as staff rooms, offices, garages, gardens, sheds may fall under this Act.

A manager or staff member, who knowingly permits, or encourages, a man to have sexual intercourse with a woman with severe learning disabilities (a 'mental defective') in a residential home within their jurisdiction may commit an offence. (Sexual Offences Act 1956 s27 (1))

Any male member of staff who has sexual intercourse with any client, within a Mental Health Act setting, may commit an offence (Mental Health Act 1959 s128 (1))

Punishments, such as depriving people of meals, would probably constitute 'wilful neglect' under the Mental Health Act 1983,s127 and contravene conditions set out under the Registered Homes Act 1984.

A person with severe learning disabilities (in legal terms 'mental defect') cannot give consent, whenever there is a consent element concerned in determining whether an offence has taken place, e.g. communications, assault, abduction, 'false imprisonment', sexual acts.

Authorizations that give power to third parties to manage the financial affairs of someone with learning disabilities are usually restricted. For example, authorization to collect a person's social security benefits (as an appointee under the Social Security Act 1987, reg.33) does not give permission to deal with earnings or gifts of money (which would require authorization under the Mental Health Act 1983, s.142). A Social Security appointee must use state benefits for the direct benefit of the claimant – maintenance to a residential unit, unwanted holidays, day-trips, or parties may not be considered as such.

Opening people's mail or intercepting phone calls, without the consent of the recipient or a court, may be an offence against the Interception of Communications Act 1985 s1 (1). This can be so even if the intent is helpful, for example intercepting cheques and putting them in a bank account.

Counselling' or 'inciting' people to do something that is unlawful is itself an offence. This may include setting up and encouraging sexual relationships that are not clearly consensual.

Most service users cannot be compelled to undergo medical treatment, which would include minor things such as taking an aspirin. There is particular confusion concerning people who are transferred from long-stay hospitals, and are under Section 8 Guardianship Orders (Mental Health Act 1983, 8 (1)). Guardianship does not sanction compulsory treatment.

Managers and staff, not directly employed by the NHS, may still be working within the Mental Health Act 1983 which makes clear a duty to care. The terms 'in-patient' and 'mental disorder' used in the Act are defined very widely, and almost certainly embrace people with learning disabilities in community settings (see Gunn 1990: 18). Service providers contracted by the NHS to provide residential care, operating a 'mental nursing home' on behalf of the NHS, are therefore covered by the Act.

Staff in residential homes are sometimes bound by the Registered Homes Act 1984. This includes a duty to notify the registration authority within 24 hours of 'any event in the home which affects the well-being of any resident; and any theft, burglary...'

Service users may sue for damages if they have not been protected from bullying, harassment and other victimization. This is a very new area of litigation, but is likely to increase, and cases may be based on events from many years before.

An unproven allegation that someone (staff member *or service user*) has committed an offence may amount to a defamation. In the case of libel (written defamation) the plaintiff need not show that there was loss or damage; this must be shown in the case of slander (verbal defamation) except when the alleged offence is imprisonable. For example, if a staff member said, 'Yuk-chung hit David', and this assault was unproven, there could be a straightforward claim for damages without the need to demonstrate that Yuk-chung's character had been affected, because assault is imprisonable.

Staff may be guilty of an offence if they impede a report to the police. Impeding a prosecution by omission (simply not reporting a crime) is not an offence. But any 'act' which intentionally impedes a prosecution may constitute an offence. A manager who, for example, instructs, verbally or in writing, that a probable crime should not be reported may commit an offence.

Staff may be dismissed lawfully if there are 'reasonable grounds' for believing that an offence has been committed, which relates to their work. The circumstances do not have to be 'proven' and a single, probable offence is sufficient grounds for dismissal.

Corroboration, by third party witnesses, of an offence is not necessary. Although it is desirable to corroborate a victim's story, a court may still convict if they believe the victim's version of events to be true. A conviction can be achieved solely on the word of a victim with learning disabilities.

The link between victimization and behaviour disabilities

This aspect of prevention is almost unique to people with learning disabilities. In service settings, much 'victimization' is, from another perspective, the 'challenging behaviour' of the perpetrator. The cause of the challenging behaviour is sometimes the victimization of that person, by another party. Breaking these victim–victimizer relationships would greatly reduce the spirals of abuse related to service settings.

The links between victimization and behaviour disabilities are widely acknowledged on a theoretical level but less evident as a basis for daily practice. Jim Mansell (1993: 4) lists among 'factors contributing to challenging behaviour': 'history of neglect, history of sexual abuse, history of physical abuse, restrictive home or day time environment which maximises confrontations'. These all represent probable offences against the people concerned.

Valerie Sinason (1992, p137) explains how victimization increases the degree of learning difficulty:

> '...if surviving [victimization] means cutting your head off [in order to forget], your intellect is destroyed. If knowing and seeing involve knowing and seeing terrible things, it is not surprising that not-knowing, becoming stupid, becomes a defence'.

She goes further and argues that victimization can cause a learning disability – 'trauma evokes handicap as a defence against the memory of physical or sexual abuse' (see also Buchanan and Oliver 1977; Cohen and Warren 1987).

The relationship between victimization and resultant behaviour disabilities is well established, and should be acknowledged through effective personal safety policies within service settings.

A review meeting had been called to discuss the 'difficult' and 'irresponsible' behaviour of Jason, pending his appearance at court for minor offences.

During the meeting he mentioned that he had been beaten up at work. Chatting about this privately afterwards he said that he had worked at McDonald's, and had, following an argument about serviettes, been pushed up against a fridge door, hit, and then locked in the fridge. He escaped by kicking his way out.

When asked if anything else like this had ever happened before he said, 'Oh, yes. When I was 14 I was raped. I had reading and writing lessons with this woman. When she wasn't there her bloke, he was 40, raped me. My ex-girlfriend told me to tell the community policeman. We had known him since we were kids. He told my dad. But my dad said we could not go to court because I wouldn't get things right in court. But the guy who did it died. He died of a heart attack. He's dead now – good job – serves him right.'

'I think this is why I'm a bit difficult now.'

Staff did not seem aware of these incidents. At his review meeting a psychologist had suggested that, because Jason did not seem satisfied with where he lived, he could simply go and live on the streets in a cardboard box, adding, 'If you can find one.' He also suggested, as Jason blamed everyone but himself for his problems, that he could go and cut his leg off and get a wooden one so that he could blame that for all his failings.

The link between minor and serious victimization

The need to prevent minor victimization has a particular significance for people with learning disabilities – vulnerability lends itself to the immediate or cumulative escalation of abuse. It is very tempting to advise victims to ignore minor incidents. Although this may be a simple way to deal with an immediate event, in the long run it may not be appropriate because minor abuse leads easily to more serious incidents.

Stories of minor abuse, which advertises vulnerability, leading to an **immediate escalation** of victimization are common. In the street there is often a pattern of verbal abuse, followed by a minor assault, damage to property or robbery, and then perhaps a major assault as events (from the perspective of the offender) get out of hand.

One woman answered her door to a man who at first attempted a 'hard sell' of catalogue goods. He went on to sexually proposition her and then, taking advantage of her confusion, stole money from her flat before departing. The parents of a man who was cheated of £2000 comment,

> 'There is often something of a slippery slope with crime against people with learning disabilities. They find money management difficult. They are often lonely and they may not always distinguish between a small "loan" or something "borrowed" and the escalation of crime.'

If people with learning disabilities are helped to recognize when they might be 'tested out' by criminals, and taught how to respond, more serious incidents may be avoided.

Minor victimization can also start a pattern of **cumulative escalation**. There are many instances in which the perpetrator has found it easy to get away with minor abuse, which creates the impression that serious offences are also possible. Links between verbal abuse by staff, assaults, and then sexual offences seem frequent. In one specific example, group of young people from a further education college were discussing Michael Murray, the manager of a residential home who had recently been convicted of raping a woman he had hypnotized. One man suddenly said,

> 'I know him. He made me go without my dinner once.'

A woman added,

> 'Yes, he used to slap people when they were naughty.'

Others then mentioned a range of similar incidents.

It is not only in the victims' interests to stop the chain of events leading from minor victimization to major crimes. It is also important that the potential perpetrators, particularly staff, are helped to curb their abuses of power at an early stage. Police often make the point that formal therapeutic help for perpetrators can usually only be triggered if victimization is reported formally to them, and the sooner the better.

'Minor' victimization can reinforce perpetrators' impressions of their power and a victim's comparative weakness, leading to more serious crimes. This highlights the importance of identifying and remedying minor injustice, especially by staff.

'Minor' offences may have serious outcomes, because of other conditions in the lives of people with disabilities. A 65-year-old woman was pushed over by another resident, in a hospital dining room. A minor incident in itself, but as a result she died, because hospital staff failed to recognize that she had a fractured skull. In a similar circumstance, an argument leading to a 'scuffle', ended with the death of a young man because the assault triggered a heart failure related to a rare heart condition that had not been diagnosed.

The effects of minor victimization are usually only noted in relation to the immediate victim. There is rarely recognition of the feelings of carers, family and friends. A string of incidents at a day centre – including hair-pulling, a bruise, and clothes torn or spoiled – was met by comments about 'not enough staff' from managers. There was no recognition of the cost of replacing damaged clothes for parents and daughter living on state benefits, or of a developing belief that staff could not be trusted. Another member of the family commented,

> 'They [the parents] went on about the bruise. Everything got on top of them. If the bruise wasn't in the Accident Book, what else wasn't in the book? What if she had been sexually abused? That wouldn't be in the book either. He [the father] said if anything like that ever happened he would take all three lives.'

The comment was made at an inquest: the parents eventually killed themselves and their daughter, leaving a note expressing their dissatisfaction with services.

The concept of 'minor' or 'serious' victimization is very subjective. If something is serious to the victim, it is serious. Cumulative 'minor' victimization might, to an individual, add up to 'serious'. To be called, 'imbecile coon' every day for five years may well have a similar effect to being mugged once. The only point at which the victimization of people with learning disabilities can safely be deemed 'minor' is in retrospect. And even then it is a judgement that should be left to the victims, not the observer.

4

Reporting

Why report to the police?

At present in the UK, there remains an assumption within service settings that reporting offences against service users to the police, should be discretionary. A study by Carolyn Allington found that of 80 staff responses concerning the 'steps they would take, or who they would inform, if they thought someone was being sexually abused', only 4 would 'inform police' (1992: 62). This non-reporting ethos is rationalised on a number of questionable grounds.

The belief that reporting 'will make things worse' is common. A recent Registered Homes Tribunal, concerning sexual abuse, concluded that residents with learning disabilities have a 'particular vulnerability' and should therefore never experience the possible 'stress of giving evidence' – evidence must 'of necessity' come from others. Whilst well-meaning, this line of thinking

- can be paternalistic, and over-protective

- can send a message to potential offenders that they will always get away with crimes against people with learning disabilities, that are not witnessed by others

- probably reflects an out-dated view of the police – in general there are now highly trained officers working in specialist units who deal daily with traumatized and vulnerable victims

- could provide the basis for a cover-up by staff

- could lead to managers giving an instruction not to report, which may be an offence of 'impeding a prosecution'.

The message for vulnerable adults [is] if you are abused and you do tell someone, one of two things could happen.

If the professionals have time, energy, resources, awareness and training for your particular client group, they will leap into action. Everybody will want to be involved – social workers, nurses, police, day centre staff, volunteer organisers. They will want to know everything about your lifestyle and your problems. They will investigate you and hold case planning meetings and completely disrupt your life as you have known it. And it is very unlikely that they will warn you of the consequences.

On the other hand, it is likely that nobody will have the time, energy or resources for you. One or two workers, probably the people you like and trust, will become upset and agitated. There will not be any money to pay for the help you need or places to go for support. You will stay in the abusive situation, only your abuser may now resent the fact that you have told someone.

In short – if you are a vulnerable adult experiencing abuse – just keep quiet.

Juliet Prager, Leeds Advocacy,
Community Living, October 1992

Individual staff sometimes feel that police involvement is an abdication of responsibility by a caring professional which may be to the detriment of a service user. Perhaps this can be true, but need it be? In many instances police are delighted to be advised by, and work with professional carers. (Of course there may be cases when it is more appropriate for no staff input, for example if staff are the alleged perpetrators.) Innovative and exemplary practice has resulted from good co-operation. Ultimately, the police (as an entity, if not always as individuals) are the professionals concerning crime.

The belief that police involvement will make a situation worse, perhaps by further traumatizing a victim, may seem a very reasonable judgement at the time an incident happens. But in retrospect the non-involvement of police can appear very different. At an inquest, where a mother and father had committed suicide, also killing their daughter who had learning disabilities, it was revealed that the mother had previously tried to kill herself and her daughter with an overdose. When this had happened, the practitioner concerned was threatened by the mother, who said that she would do the same again if he told the police. Based on his judgement of the circumstances of the moment, he did not inform the police. Subsequently he found himself relating these events at the inquest, when the daughter *had* been killed by the parents. His judgement appeared in very a different light.

It was also revealed at the inquest that the daughter had, on one occasion, returned home from her day centre with a four-inch bruise, seemingly caused by a bite. There was a photograph of this. The position was such that the injury could not have been self-inflicted. The police had not been contacted, although it is probable that an offence of causing actual bodily harm had been committed. Again, avoiding police involvement might have seemed reasonable at the time, but in the light of a suicide note from the parents, saying that 'doctors and social workers... couldn't care less', the decision appeared less reasonable. Had there had been a policy that police should always be informed when a vulnerable person was the victim of a crime, these dilemmas would not have arisen for the doctor or care staff.

Failing to report a crime because of a belief, or threat, that police involvement will worsen a situation is very questionable. Such a decision may appear negligent in the light of future, perhaps more serious, circumstances.

Staff and families often feel, perhaps because of previous experience, that the police will over-react. In one example, police were phoned because a man in a group home was running around threatening people with a butter knife. The response was a van with officers in full riot kit, and an aggressive arrest of the man. In retrospect this was inappropriate and regrettable. But officers from another force point out that the response was not so very unreasonable, in

> *The police doctor shouted at the victim and caused her to cry. She was distressed by the police interrogation which the good neighbour terminated because she not only saw the injured party getting very distraught but believed that there was a possibility of her striking one of the officers.*

Stanley Hewitt, former police officer, 1987

an area of London with a high rate of violent crime, given the report included the word 'knife'. Even a butter knife can remove someone's eye and an over-response is probably better than no response. The lesson from this situation is that the report was not made to an officer who knew whom he was dealing with. **Proper liaison with police before emergencies arise, about how incidents should be reported, is essential.**

Perhaps the most common argument against reporting is the belief that the police will not be able, or willing, to do anything because of an individual's poor witness skills and/or lack of corroborating evidence. However, it is very questionable to base a decision not to report on a guess about the response of the police. Even if there is a feeling that 'the police always ignore reports', this is no reason for not making reports and insisting, through senior officers and complaints procedures, that they are taken seriously. The way something is reported can be crucial: usually greater success is achieved by contacting more senior officers directly, especially those in domestic violence or child protection units.

When a complaint is made directly by a person with learning disabilities, the police response can range from abusive – 'Go soak your head you nutter' – to exemplary. When a man, who lives alone, suffered a burglary, police attended within ten minutes of his phone call. They took full details and even checked his shopping list to sort out what was missing from his fridge. Before leaving they contacted the council to request that the door lock was changed as soon as possible.

Staff often argue that mandatory reporting is inappropriate because particular individuals commonly make false accusations. It is only necessary to sit in a court for a few days to realize that it is not only people with learning disabilities who make false allegations! Accusations may be attention-seeking behaviour, but this should be addressed rather than ignored. Conversely, there are many instances where people thought to be 'crying wolf' are eventually vindicated.

The critical question is not whether allegations are false, but how allegations are dealt with. The service ethos should be such that there is no stigma attached to investigations and brief suspensions, and that this is a normal and expected part of caring for people with learning disabilities. One college lecturer recalls how he was accused, by a student with learning disabilities, of an assault. He was suspended for a long period, but the allegation was eventually found to be false. He feels that the student had every right to make the allegation, and that the principal was right to suspend him. His complaint is that the matter took a very long time to resolve because there was no clear policy about such situations, and that no one at the college would interview the other students who had witnessed the alleged incident because they had learning disabilities.

Had the police been called, the matter would probably have been dealt with in a few days.

The only safe policy is that all allegations are investigated, regardless of the few people who may make false allegations. Investigations and suspensions should be a normal and accepted part of being a professional, but there should be a quick and efficient procedure for investigating the circumstances of a complaint.

What will be the attitude to mandatory reporting in the future? Anyone determining policy statements for local services should be aware of changing attitudes in the UK and abroad. At least one health authority now has a policy that the police will always be involved when an allegation of an offence is against a staff member. This not only sends appropriate messages to potential offenders, but also protects staff from the half-truths and rumours which surround allegations that are never properly investigated. Other authorities follow this procedure with regard to sexual assaults.

Public attitudes are changing too. Failure to report sexual abuse at a home for children with learning disabilities in Colchester, may have appeared reasonable in 1984 when the incidents happened, but less so to a parent in 1993: 'There was a lot of questions asked about why it had taken so long. They did not seem to have an answer... I want to know exactly what happened in 1984. By the sound of it there was good cause then for a police investigation' (*Evening Gazette*, 9 September 1993: 3).

In North America, reporting to an independent agency by professionals is becoming mandatory. The Vulnerable Persons Protection Bill 1992 (218) of Alberta requires that service providers ensure that criminal abuse is reported to the law enforcement agency, and that any other abuse or neglect is reported. Legislation in Connecticut is especially interesting.

In addition to ethical and moral questions, there are pragmatic reasons for reporting to the police and pursuing cases through the courts:

- Success in the courts often depends on the police gathering evidence *immediately*. Forensic evidence, for example relating to a sexual assault, usually must be obtained within 48 hours. Photographs taken by police photographers are now a very strong part of the evidence used to prove assault. Where victim and defendant are the only witnesses to assault, cases can hinge on a police photograph of injuries, taken soon after the event.

- Criminal Injuries Compensation can only be claimed when someone is the victim of a 'violent' crime and the crime is reported to the police 'without delay'. (The identity of the offender need not be known.)

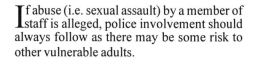

If abuse (i.e. sexual assault) by a member of staff is alleged, police involvement should always follow as there may be some risk to other vulnerable adults.

Sexual abuse and adults with learning disabilities a framework for practice guide-lines, Whoriskey, Green and McKay 1993.

WHO MUST REPORT
Included in the list of mandated reporters are physicians, nurses, dentists, dental hygienists, occupational and physical therapists, psychologists, social workers, teachers, speech pathologists, police officers, and any person paid for caring for persons in any facility.

FAILURE TO REPORT
If a mandated reporter fails to report suspected abuse, and this is discovered in a subsequent investigation, the person or persons are subject to a fine...the mandated reporter [must] ensure that a report has been made even if they themselves do not make the call or submit the form. A mandated reporter has not fulfilled his or her obligation until the Abuse Investigation Division has received the report.

PROTECTION OF THE INFORMANT
...a person who makes a good faith report of abuse is immune from any civil or criminal liability. He or she cannot be sued in civil or criminal court by the person they accused of committing the abuse. Anyone who 'hinders or endangers' any person reporting abuse is also subject to a fine.
In addition, the law provides protection from reprisal or discharge from one's place of employment for making a good faith report of abuse or neglect.

Connecticut General Statutes, 19a-458 (1985), described by Furey and Haber (1989: 136).

- Criminal Injuries Compensation does not cover claims under £1000. Compensation under £1000 can only be achieved through a court.

- Whilst the police cannot keep official records of unproven allegations, they do maintain an informal knowledge of suspected offenders. This can influence the seriousness with which they treat subsequent reports. At a period when economic constraints lead to strict prioritization of police resources, the importance of this should not be underestimated.

- Police involvement can help reinforce crime prevention lessons for victims. In an instance in which £2000 went missing from a man's building society account, the local police were very helpful, but it was decided not to pursue the case because evidence was weak. Despite this, the man's parent concludes:

    'I think the police had an entirely beneficial effect on John. Nice as they were, they made him realise it was a serious matter and he had to take some responsibility for looking after his own affairs.'

- Staff protect themselves against allegations of negligence or of impeding a prosecution if they make a report.

- Perpetrators cannot usually be helped unless their actions are formally recognized. A conviction can sometimes make funds available for help, that would not be available otherwise. In cases where a degree of compulsion is required to make someone address a personal problem (e.g. relating to alcohol or drugs abuse) the courts may be the only way of achieving this.

There is a trend towards mandatory reporting by staff to the police, and of ensuring the protection of staff who report. The crucial question should not be whether or not to report to the police but how the police and CPS then respond.

Fear of reprisals against staff is another strong deterrent to reporting. Discussion about 'whistle-blowing', and recent Department of Health guidelines which permit sanctions against staff who 'go public', are sometimes misinterpreted by staff. The guidelines concern staff reporting general dissatisfaction about services to the public. They do not suggest that crimes should not be reported to the police. Staff contracts or comments from managers which suggest that direct reporting to the police is not permitted could be unlawful, because they might represent an 'act with intent to impede' the prosecution of an offence.

I have seen residents cry because they have been shouted at, or told off or neglected and because the care staff need a job they are frightened to speak out.

Care Weekly, 21 October 1993: 7

For staff who fear reprisals from employers there is a new organization, Public Concern at Work, which includes 'the abuse of vulnerable people' in its remit. It will pursue matters confidentially at first and if necessary protect staff from reprisals. It operates a phoneline.

Finally, the most important argument for reporting is put by Valerie Sinason of the Tavistock Centre (London),

> 'Often when children and adults with learning disabilities are referred for therapy I find out that it's not therapy they've needed, it's justice. Many adults have been referred because their case didn't get to court, or because the police weren't interested in interviewing them, and their despair that their experience hasn't counted is what's led to their emotionally disturbed behaviour.' (Channel 4: *Breaking the Silence,* June 1994).

There is an inherent human need for justice, which is no different for people with learning disabilities.

Public Concern at Work
42 Kingsway,
London WC2B 6EN
Tel 0171- 404 6609

Confidentiality

Among psychologists and those providing counselling the question of client confidentiality is always raised as a reason for not reporting. The *Code of Conduct for Psychologists* (1985) of the British Psychological Society (BPS) is helpful for Society members and others.

In the Code 'appropriate third parties' (which could mean the police in the case of a crime) should be informed when a past or potential offence is mentioned, if the 'safety or interests' of a service user or others 'may be threatened'. There is no mention of balancing the seriousness of the 'threat' against the probable outcome of breaching confidentiality. Put more practically:

- a threat of any offence, by or against a client, should be reported to an 'appropriate third party'

- a past offence, by or against a client, which might suggest the possibility of future offences happening, should be reported.

The BPS Code does not take specific account of people who may be particularly vulnerable.

If a person with learning disabilities stated that he or she had been victimized, the greater likelihood of a threat to interests or safety should be taken into account.

Confidentiality Psychologists shall: in exceptional circumstances, where there is sufficient evidence to raise serious concern about the safety or interests of recipients of services, or about others who may be threatened by the recipient's behaviour, take such steps as are judged necessary to inform appropriate third parties without prior consent after first consulting an experienced and disinterested colleague, unless the delay caused by seeking this advice would involve a significant risk of life or health;

A Code of Conduct for Psychologists,
British Psychological Society 1985

It is very difficult to conceive of any circumstances, when actual or potential crimes are mentioned, which may not pose some form of threat to the interests or safety of a person with learning disabilities or others. The conclusion must be that confidentiality will be breached when offences are mentioned.

All service managers will know individual professionals whom they would trust absolutely to make a sound decision about reporting. But policy statements must take account of the majority, most of whom are not known personally, some of whom may be inexperienced employees. One of the most bizarre excuses for not reporting a minor assault in the street came from a psychologist. He explained that as the victim had been abused, as a child, by his father, he therefore 'expects' abuse from staff and others – he 'attracts' victimization, and reporting would be inappropriate.

In accord with British Psychological Association guidelines, any mention of criminal offences should be reported to an appropriate third party, regardless of issues of confidentiality, unless there is absolute certainty that no person's safety or interests will ever be threatened as a result.

Professionals who are uncomfortable with the need to breach confidentiality might consider

- making it clear, before counselling starts, that confidentiality does not apply when discussion relates to an offence

- at the moment a client starts to mention anything that may relate to a crime, reminding them that this may not be treated confidentially

- how to explain to clients why confidentiality must be broken. This might include: the safety or interests of the client; the duty of care towards others; public interest. Victims can also be assured that the police will be told about their wish not to prosecute.

Victims who do not want to report

Perhaps the most difficult circumstance is when a victim explicitly does not want a report to be made to the police, particularly if it is felt that the decision is not based on a complete understanding of what has happened, of the likely consequences of this decision, and what is 'normal' in such circumstances. In one example, police were unable to bring charges against a gang, who sexually assaulted a young man in the street, simply because he was afraid to identify them. A prior knowledge of the outcome of reporting, reassurance about protection, and the offer of moving to a new location may have overcome this problem.

Sometimes the reasons for not wishing to report are very simple. One victim, who was punched in the mouth and required stitches, said, when asked about why he did not want police involvement,

> 'Because you have to describe people and things and I'm no good at that. The hospital's better – they don't ask.'

Other circumstances are more complicated. One Muslim woman was very reluctant to report a sexual assault which happened over a holiday period. She had refused to travel abroad to her family home, with her parents, because she wanted to spend the holiday with her friends in the UK. Her parents had been annoyed and 'said something like this would happen'. In addition the victim's mother was very ill and she thought that 'it would kill her' to know. Other cultural

> *In my job I tell people to complain all the time. But then I go home and want to complain about my daughter's school and she says 'please don't complain'.*

Inspection Officer,
Care Weekly, 21 October 1993: 7.

> *I was raped by a day centre staff member. I did not take my case to the police because I was told that I would not get anywhere with it and not to bother.*

prejudices could contribute to a fear of reporting, for example that women are inherently to blame for any form of unwanted sexual contact.

Previous negative experiences with the police often underlie a reluctance to report, and problems are not necessarily caused intentionally. In a discussion about personal protection a very confident woman who had previously been asked to try to identify someone from police files stated with great vehemence, 'I wouldn't report a rape because, when I went to the police to look at pictures, they didn't say, "thank you". They make you feel guilty if you can't identify the person. They didn't even say thanks for me taking the morning off work.'

A woman who reported a sexual assault on a bus, met with cursory interest from police, because there was a delay of a day. She commented,

> 'No one seemed to want to help. I don't know if they believed me or not. I don't think it was fair how I was treated.'

An extremely competent man explained a reluctance to talk to police because when officers attended an incident where another man was threatening him with hands round his throat, the police response was, 'You two, stop behaving like children.'

Intimidation by staff may also deter reporting. In Scotland, at a High Court hearing after which a care assistant was jailed for sexually assaulting two men and two women, the court was told that the victims believed that if they reported they would be sent back to 'mental hospital'. Staff, paid carers and volunteers have a clear power relationship with people with learning disabilities; hence the need for mandatory reporting now acknowledged in policy guidelines, for example in those from Greenwich Social Services. However, the Greenwich guidelines are less clear cut concerning alleged offences by family members or other carers.

Whilst the victims 'have the right not to report' to the police, this does not necessarily bind any other person who shares the knowledge of an offence. The Greenwich guidelines unfortunately make no reference to policy when the offender also has learning disabilities: a very common situation.

An increase in awareness about sexual assault by known people and domestic violence against women is very relevant here. It is now realised that a reluctance to report is a major feature of the power of the perpetrator, that power relationships are ever present in families, and that a report against a victim's wishes is often met with relief because the responsibility for the decision has been removed from them.

WHEN TO REFER
All allegations involving a member of staff, paid carer or volunteer must be reported regardless of the wishes of the client. In these situations clients will need sensitive and careful support and this policy will need to be carefully explained.

Greenwich Social Services:
Policy Guidelines 1993, 7.2

Staff need to recognise that if the perpetrator is a family member or another carer (as distinct from a paid carer) the victim may not wish their disclosure to be further investigated or to report it to the Police. Adults who are able to consent [i.e. are not in law a 'mental defect'] ultimately have the right not to report the matter to the Police but the member of staff must report all disclosed incidents to their immediate Line Manager and the wishes of the client should be recorded. The decision not to report to the Police should be talked through with great care with the client. The implications/possible on-going risk to the individual, and possibly to others, should be fully explored and discussed with the Principal Resource Manager.

Greenwich Social Services:
Policy Guidelines, 1993, 7.3

'I did not tell anyone about what Mary had said about the pottery teacher at the day centre touching her up. She told me in a confidential therapy session, and said not to tell the police.' (Psychologist)

There are two **separate** questions to decide:

1.   *Should the psychologist breach confidentiality?*

The answer is clearly, yes. The incident could be repeated leading to more serious assaults, i.e. the 'interests' or 'safety' of Mary and others could be 'threatened' (see BPS Code).

2.   *Should Mary's wishes be the deciding factor in whether the psychologist reports to the police?*

The decision should be discussed with Mary, to help her develop a **full understanding** of all possible outcomes. This should include the safety of other people, and the knowledge that telling the police does not necessarily lead to a prosecution if it is against the victim's wishes.

If her judgement cannot be based on a full understanding of outcomes, it is reasonable for staff to **substitute judgement.** For example, if Mary thinks that everyone who is taken away by the police ends up in prison, a staff member could judge what decision she would make if she realised that this was not the case.

If, with full understanding, Mary still insists on not reporting, the decision of staff members rests on whether what they have been told relates to their **duty to care**, towards the client and others. In almost every circumstance there will a duty to care, which will extend beyond the individual victim.

If there is clearly no duty to care, the decision can be made on the basis of **conscience**, i.e. in the way it would if a friend or neighbour had told of being victimized. But this circumstance would be very rare when a formal caring relationship exists.

In the example given, there is an obvious duty to care, which also has a broader social interest. The victim could be told that the incident must be reported for the safety of herself and others, but that the police will be told of her wish for no prosecution.

Staff are often not aware that the police are now more inclined to take the victim's views into account when deciding how to proceed with a case, especially in domestic matters (not least because the prosecution usually requires the cooperation of the victim). The CPS may also take into account the victim's wishes.

The concept of 'social interest' should also be taken into account when considering a request not to inform the police. If there is a conflict between an individual's wishes and the interests of society, the latter, in judicial decisions, is given preference. For example, a benevolent woman may not want a prosecution against someone who stole her bike, because the bike has been recovered. But the greater interest of protecting other bike owners might require that some action be taken. The 'duty to care', in relation to a whole client group, is a form of 'social interest'.

It is useful to decide, with police, an outline policy when victims do not want a prosecution against offenders. The critical question should be the form police action takes in this circumstance, not the decision to report or not.

Service users should be aware that staff have a duty to care and therefore must report anything that might threaten the safety or interests of themselves or others.

The decision to report is stressful for anyone. Victim Support (see local phone book) is an excellent source of general support, but two other strategies may be especially helpful for people with learning disabilities. Firstly, the use of a lay 'Citizen Advocate', which might be arranged through a local Citizen Advocacy Scheme.

Secondly, a 'Circle of Support' might assist an individual to take a decision to report, and help with the practical and emotional implications. Circles of Support take many forms. In outline, a circle is a group of people, chosen by the individual which, with a facilitator (who leads if necessary and ensures that 'things get done'), has the necessary range of practical skills to achieve a desired goal and the human skills to provide support as needed.

If a local citizen advocacy scheme is not known of, contact:

Citizen Advocacy Alliance
Douglas House
26 Sutton Court Road
Sutton
Surrey
SM1 4SY

Tel: 0181- 643 7111

More information and help can be obtained from:

Circles Network
6 Stanbury Avenue
Fishponds
Bristol
BS16 5AN

Ensuring effective reporting

The starting point for ensuring that offences are reported is to teach people with learning disabilities to recognize crime before they are victims – obvious, but frequently overlooked! Crime awareness should include recognition and conceptualization of crime and how to get justice. If people do not recognize that an event is a crime, or perhaps do not have the vocabulary to describe it as such, even the most cooperative police efforts can be frustrated.

Language, especially vocabulary, is a key to conceptualizing crime and reporting effectively. Staff working with people with learning disabilities might usefully analyse the confusion that their own jargon can create. It may be very difficult for a person with learning disabilities (or anyone else) to understand that,

> 'disclosed physical abuse by a client with challenging behaviour'

might translate as

> 'said Fred hit him'.

The concept of proof is also vital. This includes corroboration ('Jane saw Fred hit me'), coinciding events that clarify a time scale ('Fred hit me after we watched the News') and other evidence ('Fred hit me with this spoon').

Frustration often arises when recurring victimization is difficult to prove, for example verbal abuse and minor assaults from school-children. One solution is to help victims to keep an accurate diary of events, with details of times, places and description (perhaps with drawings). This provides more convincing evidence when approaching police (or perhaps a headteacher), and the process may reveal useful patterns, for example, of a specific time or day, which can help trace perpetrators. If nothing else it helps victims to have a sense that they are 'doing something.'

Tape recorders, cameras and video recorders can similarly assist reporting. The stories of victims, injuries, incidents, and settings can be recorded. Staff at one Day Centre reported an immediate cessation of harassment from local school children after a filming session (with staff) at a local bus stop.

Mary returned home having been treated at hospital for a cut forehead. She said she had fallen.

At home the following day poor mobility was noticed in her left arm and extensive bruising was discovered. She eventually agreed to return to casualty for further examination, but still stated that she had fallen. At this point it was also noted that her handbag was missing. I then reported the incident to the police on the off-chance that any witnesses had reported anything, but as Mary would not say anything other than that she had fallen they could do little else.

The following day the police visited the home with Mary's handbag, which had been found in the possession of two youths in the process of mugging another person. The assumption was then made that this is what happened to Mary.

She still doesn't talk about the incident however hard we have worked to ensure she is secure and confident enough to do so. In fact she becomes quite angry when the subject is brought up. We have had no further contact with the police, so we don't know if these youths admitted anything or not.

Home manager

 Jenny Speaks Out and *Bob Tells All* are illustrated booklets to help people with learning disabilities recognise and report sexual offences. Available from:

Division of Psychiatry of Disability
St George's Hospital Medical School
Cranmer Terrace
London SW17 0RE

Once victims understand when and how to report, the main reason for reports not reaching the police is the linear, 'chain' nature of reporting routes within service settings. If one link in the chain of reporting fails, there are rarely alternatives. There is no reason why reporting routes for service users should relate to formal line-management structures. In one case, serious on-going assaults only came to light because a student on placement told her tutor who alerted the local press, from where the police picked up the story. Area managers need to ensure that potential victims have a variety of reporting routes, not least because perpetrators, or those wishing to protect them, often create the missing link in reporting chains themselves.

The ways in which perpetrators can use their power to prevent detection should not be underestimated. The report of an independent inquiry into circumstances leading to the conviction of a day centre manager, in Wales, for sexual offences concluded,

> 'One of the ways Mr Maidment was able to create and maintain a reign of abuse was to control the flow of information in and out of the centre.

> 'Maidment could maintain control over incidents which might have led to his detection because he was a "respectable" member of the local community, working in youth and football clubs, and serving as local Mayor for one year. The trial judge commented,

> '"I suppose that it was hardly surprising that this mentally defective woman was disbelieved, in view of the defendant's character as it was known at the time".'

In retrospect staff may recognise numerous ways in which senior staff who have victimized clients have used power relationships to hide their actions. Influence over promotions, appointments, training opportunities, equipment, who goes on overseas holidays, and every aspect of the daily running of a centre or home, can all be part of the pattern of control which deters reporting.

Front-line police can also represent the 'missing link' in reporting chains. There are countless stories from people with learning disabilities about their reports being ignored. In some instances 'no further action' may well be justifiable, but the number of times this is mentioned indicates a general problem. If nothing else, the reasons for not investigating further are often not clearly explained. In one case a man complained to officers of what he saw as assaults by staff. The police spoke only to the manager of the home without meeting the complainant. The incidents were simply explained away by terms such as 'control and restraint procedures'.

Managers should ensure that service users have access to reporting 'webs' rather than reporting 'chains'.

A complaint to the police can be outlined in writing with the following information.

Who is suspected of committing the offence? (Name, address or other identifying details, e.g. 'he is from the newspaper shop')

What happened – where, when, and how?

Who else saw it?

What law has been broken, if you know? If you believe that European law has also been broken, mention this (see Chapter Six).

Why do you want a prosecution? You should mention
- the effects on the victim
- that there is a 'public interest' beyond the victim, e.g. 'the man who did it is often alone with lots of women, so he might do it again.'

In some circumstances, if the police do not need to collect evidence quickly, a letter might be appropriate. This can be taken to the local police station or sent to the Chief Constable (see phone book under 'Police' for address):

The Chief Constable.

Dear Sir or Madam
I want to complain about some boys from Wensley School, 12 Downsend Drive, Burley.

Every Monday, at about 4.00pm, four of these boys have hit us and shouted at us when we are waiting at the bus stop outside the garage in Wensley Road. Last week they hit Mary badly and smashed Talik's Walkman and said we were fucking cretins which made us frightened.

Last Monday the woman from the house with a red front door saw them and told them to stop

We think this is an assault and damage, and against the Public Order law.

We want you to do something because Mary's arm still hurts and Talik has not got enough money for another Walkman, and we are all afraid to wait at the bus stop on Mondays.

We don't think children should get away with this because they will do it to other people if they do. And they will go on doing it when they are big.

Yours faithfully

Services should avoid linear 'chain' reporting routes.

One broken link can block a report to police who will take appropriate action.

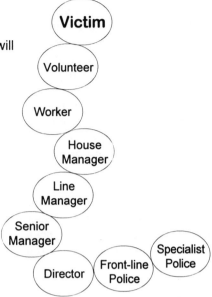

Instead there should be a 'reporting web', which does not preclude direct reporting to senior police, senior management and inspection units.

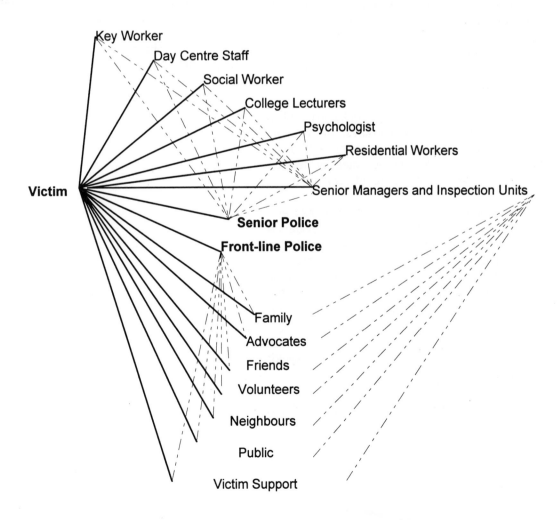

There are a number of examples of good practice to overcome the problems of 'chain' reporting routes. In one Social Services district, all service users have a preprinted 'help' card which identifies them by a number. All they need do is post it and a senior manager will investigate. Some authorities insist that the telephone in residential settings must be in a place where residents can use it without fear of being overheard. Homes must display a 'help' number by the phone (perhaps using an automatic dialling button) and residents must be regularly reminded how to use it. The name and phone number of the Community Police Officer can be displayed, and/or training about 999 calls given. It might be good practice to try to ensure that at least one resident in every residential unit can conceptualize crime and has the communication and other skills needed to report clearly.

In a few instances, inspections include regular private discussions or drawing sessions with residents to discover the 'bad things' about their lives. The address of Social Services Independent Inspection Units is sometimes made known to all carers.

'Hi-tech' methods of providing reporting routes, substantiating reports, and crime prevention could be more fully explored. One approach for people who have difficulty communicating might be the use of personal alarms which are worn like a wrist watch, of the type available for elderly people who live alone. In Enfield and Limehouse (London) a personal alarm system for vulnerable women alerts a district council control room. In West and South Yorkshire the police give pre-programmed Vodaphones, which will dial the police instantly, to women who feel vulnerable to victimization.

A more simple, preventive measure is to put locks on people's bedrooms. For people who cannot manage keys, card systems are already available, and it is likely that improving technology will soon produce locks that could be activated by devices such as electronic bracelets in the manner of car alarms.

Video recording in service settings, as used in buses and shopping precincts, is another possibility, to provide evidence when physical or sexual assaults are alleged. Obviously this raises ethical questions and goes against ideas of ordinary living, but public opinion, balancing civil liberties and personal safety, is changing fast concerning other community settings. Future discussion might consider a range of approaches, for example:

- video surveillance which was only accessible to senior management, under strict guidelines

- video surveillance with the full agreement of all those concerned (in general, staff might welcome this as it would protect them from false allegations)

Useful advice and addresses for carers, parents, and people with learning disabilities is given in *Who can I tell? Blowing the whistle on sexual abuse*, from

NAPSAC
Department of Learning Disabilities
Floor E, South Block
University Hospital
Nottingham
NG7 2UH

Tel 0115-970 9987

- the possible use of cameras only in the quasi-public areas of group homes and day centres (hallways, staff rooms, gardens).

The use of video is very contentious, and these ideas are not proposals, simply lines of discussion. However, it is worth noting that in many service settings video surveillance is already in operation for general security reasons, which could well be used as evidence in court in relation to an offence against a member.

Attitude and tradition are other, more general, reasons for reporting failures. Sometimes service managers do not acknowledge that anyone, including staff and service users, has the right to report anything they like directly to the police at any time. Managers who discourage direct reporting should question their motives, not least because they may be guilty of impeding a prosecution.

Policy statements can discourage direct reporting because of their complexity. At a conference about the abuse of people with learning disabilities, a young worker asked simply, 'If a client is raped, what should I do? Use the guidelines or phone the police?' There should be no question of 'or' in this circumstance. Delays in reporting, because of complex referral procedures, often mean that police cannot gather evidence effectively. **The tradition of staff and service users not reporting directly to the police should be questioned.**

The police and Crown Prosecution Service (CPS) response

Staff often complain that the police do not treat reports of offences against people with learning disabilities seriously, and there are numerous stories from carers and victims supporting this view. But before drawing any conclusion it is worth considering the norm for reporting generally: only half the cases reported to the police are then formally recorded.

Non-recording may be for very good reasons – an instance of abuse or harassment may not technically be an offence. However, station officers who wish to maintain a high 'clear up' rate might be tempted to avoid recording reports that will not lead to convictions or cautions. A report made to police – that an angler with learning disabilities almost drowned after two 'laughing yobs' pushed him into a freezing, fast-flowing river – was initially written up by a young officer as an assault, but she was then told to fill out an 'incident' report instead. The result – yet another example of crime against people with learning disabilities becomes 'invisible' within official sources.

Managers tried to hide sex abuse

Council staff have tried to conceal evidence of abuse and neglect of mentally handicapped adults living in council-run residences in South London.

Social Services managers at Southwark Council have attempted to prevent concerned staff reporting conditions at the homes to an independent audit team...[which] was asked to audit standards of care in six residential homes after an internal inquiry last year into allegations of physical and sexual abuse... Three staff were sacked as a result of the inquiry. The home has since closed...
'Parents...found evidence of injuries being sustained by their children while at Lordship Lane, which were recorded in files but not communicated to them at the time,' the report says...
It adds: 'During the audit, evidence was found that at least some staff had been instructed not to complain or criticise the service. Some staff did seem frightened to answer questions. The audit team had no doubt the these staff genuinely believed that management intended to suppress critical views...

Observer, 6 February 1994: 2

The police say that sometimes they do not respond appropriately because of the jargon used by professionals. Senior officers will also advise that desk staff (now sometimes civilians with little training) are not always the best people to contact. Desk officers, in the words of an inspector, 'Are often on the desk as a punishment for messing something up!'

Staff need to know exactly who to contact in a police station – a named officer, the child protection team or domestic violence unit. Reports need to be free of jargon, and stress urgency if appropriate.

Officers who seem reluctant to interview witnesses because they have learning disabilities should be directed towards, 'Witnesses who have mental handicaps' (Bull and Cullen 1992) available from the Crown Office, Edinburgh. A publication from the Roeher Institute in Canada, *No more victims: a manual to guide the police in addressing the sexual abuse of people with mental handicap* (1992), provides perspective from another country.

If front-line police officers do not respond appropriately, staff should immediately contact the senior officer on duty at the station concerned. It can be very effective to quote exactly which law may have been broken. For example, ordinary police officers will not be used to dealing with 'ill-treatment' and 'neglect' within the Mental Health Act 1983 s127. They may not immediately consider laws of 'false imprisonment' in a care setting, nor the Public Order Act 1986 if they believe a building to be entirely a dwelling. They are unlikely to be aware of the powers of a Justice of the Peace, within the Registered Homes Act 1984 to make an urgent order cancelling the registration of a Registered Home if there is a 'serious risk to the life, health, or well-being of the residents'.

The police decision to recommend to the CPS that a prosecution would be appropriate is sometimes based on referral guides which list the basic elements of an offence. It is helpful to ask the officer concerned to discuss these elements because it is easy to overlook small aspects of an incident which could be deciding factors in the police decision to prosecute.

This referral guidance varies between police regions. In itself this appears very questionable as it could lead to the law being applied differently from region to region. In one region the guidance form concerning 'False Imprisonment' posed a particular problem because it required that an 'injury' had been suffered in addition to the imprisonment. This is contradicted by *Halsbury's Laws* which states that, 'False imprisonment is...an indictable offence, **even if no violence is used**' (Vol. 45: 610).

Problems caused by jargon.

'The police took four days to respond when a woman had been raped, so all the evidence was gone.' (Social worker)

'What did you say when you reported this?'

'I phoned 999 and said, "A person with learning disabilities has just disclosed that she had been abused".'

999 calls are not answered by people who are necessarily likely to understand that 'learning disabilities', 'disclosed' and 'abused' implies that a woman has just been raped. If 999 is the only option, state in plain English what has happened, and the urgency (or not) of the matter.

How to record an initial complaint.

1. Record in writing the exact words

2. Record as soon as possible

3. If possible get the complainant to read and sign it.

4. Sign it yourself and include the time date and location

5. Do not question the complainant unduly.

Advice to staff from Detective Inspector Greg Barry, Vulnerable Victims Unit, Kent Police.

For a victim with learning disabilities, to stress psychological injury caused by the trauma of imprisonment may be sufficient to meet this 'injury' element, but this would be very difficult to prove to an investigating officer at the time of the report. There are examples in which a person has been locked in a room for a day without food and water, yet suffered no visible injury.

Regional procedures, providing guidance to police officers about the decision to prosecute, should be monitored nationally to ensure that, (i) the law is correctly and unambiguously interpreted, and (ii) the advice does not mitigate against the equitable achievement of justice for vulnerable people because of the special nature of some of the offences that they commonly suffer.

There is inconsistency concerning the requirement for an 'appropriate adult' to help *victims and witnesses* with learning disabilities. In Scotland, unpublished guidelines recommend an 'appropriate adult' for suspects, victims and witnesses. In England and Wales it is generally concluded that the Police and Criminal Evidence Act 1984 (PACE) Notes for Guidance requirement is only in relation to suspects, but at least one police authority teaches recruits that it also concerns victims and witnesses. **The role of an appropriate adult for victims and witnesses should be reviewed to ensure consistency within the UK.**

Police sometimes maintain that they cannot bring prosecutions for common assault unless the victim makes a complaint. They should be referred to *Pivoting v. Willoughby [1905] 2 KB 294*, which established that a third party can instigate proceedings if the victim is incapable of doing this and/or is under the control of the perpetrator. There is an illogical police/court tradition in the UK that considers a verbal complaint from an adult victim to be a necessity (e.g. someone stating in person to an officer or the court, 'He hit me'), yet in the case of murder, or even serious injury, there is no personal complaint, and a case is instigated by the police on behalf of the victim.

Similarly, police sometimes maintain that a victim's story must be corroborated. This is incorrect, except concerning treason, perjury, procuration or speeding. If the victim and defendant are the only witnesses, a court can convict simply on the basis of whose story is most believable. Courts seem progressively more inclined to believe the evidence of victim-witnesses, even if young or inarticulate, when there is no possibility of other witnesses.

Police may also need reminding that, simply because a victim cannot communicate, this does not mean that a case cannot be heard in court. Even when the plea is 'not guilty', the victim does not necessarily have to give evidence. In one case of rape, a successful conviction was achieved after a woman's advocate was allowed to give evidence on her behalf (Heptinstall 1994: 8).

> *You see, what you're saying to me is basically a crime without a victim... unless a victim comes forward, there's not a lot we can do. And if they've beaten the shit out of her no one's gonna come forward.*

Policeman responding to a report that a woman with mental health problems had just been seriously assaulted in the street.

Independent on Sunday, 24 July 1994: 21.

Crime cannot be neglected or ignored...The public interest must come first, but the harm done to a victim is the usual cause of action and in considering the public interest no one should overlook or disregard the interests of the victim...Victims should always be treated fairly and without adverse discrimination. Consistently with this, the services will give particular consideration to victims who are especially vulnerable such as children, victims of sexual or violent crime, and those who are severely shocked by their experience.

The police should respond to complaints of crime as promptly as the circumstances allow, with courtesy and attention...The police should outline to the victim the investigatory process. They should aim to ensure that he or she is told of significant developments in the case...

Victims's Charter, Home Office 1990: 8–9

71

Many officers are not aware that, although video links in courts cannot be used for adults as they can for children, officers do use video recordings of victim-witness statements for other purposes. A video can persuade the CPS that an individual has the skills to be an adequate witness, and to convince suspects of the wisdom of making a guilty plea, which saves the trauma of a court appearance for the victim.

Victim Support (see local phone book) might help if the police or CPS seem reluctant to pursue a case. If there is general dissatisfaction with the police response to a reported crime, a formal complaint can be made to the Chief Constable (see phone book under POLICE for the address). If a delay might interfere with achieving justice, stress the urgency, and use a fax. If the response is still unsatisfactory, contact the Police Complaints Authority, but only after the internal police procedures have been tried. Complaints must be against a particular officer(s). Complaints can be pursued by someone other than the complainant providing there is permission (if possible written) from the complainant. Ultimately it is possible that a civil action may be possible against police who have blocked a prosecution unreasonably.

Victim Support
National Office
Cranmer House
39 Brixton Road
London SW9 6DZ

Fax 0171-582 5712
Tel 0171-735 9166

Police Complaints Authority
10 Great George Street
London
SW1P 3AE

If the police base their decision not to proceed on a guess about the likely response of the Crown Prosecution Service (CPS), insisting that a case is referred will usually be successful – the police have nothing to lose by passing on the responsibility for a decision and a lot to lose if they block a case unreasonably. If this fails, the CPS can be contacted directly (see phone book for address).

If the CPS block a case, they can be asked for clear reasons. If they conclude that the victim is an inadequate witness without meeting the individual concerned (which is often the case!), this gives grounds for further pressure and perhaps a complaint to the Director of Public Prosecutions at the central office of the CPS. Some cases concerning victims with learning disabilities, false imprisonment for example, may be outside the daily experience of the CPS.

The *Code for Crown Prosecutors* is a public document which outlines how the CPS will reach a decision. This can be obtained from

Information Branch
Crown Prosecution Service
50 Ludgate Hill
London
EC4M 7EX

Tel 0171-273 8152

Whilst ultimately there is no right to prosecution, it is possible to ask for a judicial review if the *process* by which a CPS or police decision has been made seems unlawful (see Ashton and Ward 1992: 156), i.e. if a decision is

- made in a way that is procedurally incorrect (eg if the police carried out no investigation of an alleged offence; if the CPS did not act in accord with their own Code of Practice)

- unreasonable or irrational – attention has been paid to irrelevant matters, or relevant matters have not been considered (e.g. the CPS has concluded that a victim would not be a good witness without meeting the person or getting a professional opinion).

- contrary to the rules of natural justice.

A judicial review is sought by written application through the High Court, but legal assistance is usual.

Ultimately a complaint to the Home Secretary, either independently or through an MP might be appropriate. This is particularly relevant when the police and CPS have clearly followed their own rules, but a change in law or regulations might be needed to improve the justice system. There are many avenues of complaint if the police or CPS do not respond appropriately. Even if the outcome may not redress an immediate injustice, a complaint may make things better for others in the future.

For help to report and take a case to court, concerning victims with learning disabilities, contact

VOICE
P.O. Box 238
Derby DE1 9JN

Tel 01332 519872

73

5

Using the Courts

It seems that few cases concerning people with learning disabilities reach the courts. Some, it appears, are inappropriately blocked by the police or CPS on the basis of a stereotyped view of the abilities of people with learning disabilities. But it is helpful to view the number of cases, concerning victims with learning disabilities, that are not followed up, in the light of what happens to cases generally. Of every 100 offences committed, only 3 end up with court convictions. In 1992 the CPS did not pursue 14 per cent of cases referred by police. Victims should be made aware of this general situation, as there is often a belief that a report to the police will automatically lead to a successful court case, and that it is the victim's fault if it does not. However, some cases do succeed, and the success rate seems to be increasing.

Private prosecutions

If it is clear that an offence has been committed, and that this could be proved, but police and/or the CPS refuse to take action, there is a little-used method of starting a prosecution privately in a magistrates' court (Magistrates' Courts Act 1952, s 1). In outline the process involves:

- making certain that there is a *prima facie* (face value) offence

- contacting the local magistrates' court to ask about the local procedure for issuing private summonses

- attending before magistrates to get the summons issued. The bench will ask for an outline of the case ('laying an information'). It is not necessary to prove the case, but the magistrates (advised by the clerk) will establish that there is a *prima facie* case to answer.

The guilty verdict on an instructor who sexually abused people with learning disabilities at a Wiltshire training centre last week marked a small step forward for campaigners.

During the week-long trial at Swindon Crown Court, four people with learning disabilities gave evidence of indecent assault inflicted on them by 57-year-old instructor, Norman Richardson... Last week the jury found him guilty of seven charges of indecent assault on two women with learning disabilities and a member of staff...

Wiltshire social services director Ray Jones said Richardson had used deviousness, threats, and intimidation to control the people he was abusing...

From the start, the SSD recognised the disabilities in bringing a case like this to court, not least in preparing the trainees for a wait of nearly two years before the trial.

Each of the trainees likely to give evidence was supported and counselled by specially trained staff, pretrial visits were made to the courts and the court processes were explained...

While at the trial, special arrangements were made so the trainees were not kept waiting. The judge ordered the barristers to take off their wigs and screens were put around the witness box. After the trial the trainees were counselled ...

Community Care, November 1992: 7

If a case fails the complainant may be expected to pay the costs of the defense and of issuing a summons, if he or she has the means to do so. (For more information about DIY legal action see Pritchard 1992: 986, 1005).

A private summons has a number of advantages. At the initial hearing, magistrates will only be concerned with whether or not a *prima facie* offence has been committed. They are unlikely to withhold permission to serve a summons on the grounds of potential witness disabilities, and, unlike the CPS, they will not consider the cost of a prosecution when making a decision. In fact, magistrates specifically must not withhold permission for a summons because of 'extraneous and extra-judicial matters'. If there is a clear *prima facie* case, magistrates can be 'compelled' to issue a summons (Halsbury's Laws Vol 29, para 321). Basic legal questions will be determined by the court clerk so a solicitor is not necessary at this stage. Legal help may be needed at a later hearing and Legal Aid is not available for private prosecutions, a Law Centre may take up a case free, or be interested to pursue a case for a modest fee in the interests of equitable justice.

If the magistrates commit a private prosecution to the Crown Court, the CPS will automatically take over. If the CPS remains convinced that there is no possibility of success it will offer no evidence to the Crown Court and the case will be dismissed, but the CPS would need to explain its decision. It may therefore be worth ensuring that minor offences are expressed in such a way that the magistrates are more likely to hear the case (summary trial). For example, magistrates are likely to hear a 'common assault' but they may refer 'assault causing actual bodily harm' (when the skin is marked) to the Crown Court.

It might be difficult for a private individual to pursue a case in this way because of the possible cost. Even if private funds are available, a civil case would probably be a more productive route because of the lower burden of proof.

Statutory bodies, voluntary organizations, and campaigning organizations should consider private prosecution if the police or CPS block a case unreasonably, because this could set precedents for criminal proceedings in the future and directly challenge questionable police and CPS practice.

Support for vulnerable witnesses

Assistance for vulnerable victim-witnesses at courts is improving. A formal 'witness support' scheme extended to 78 courts at the end of 1994, run by paid co-ordinators who train volunteers. However, those supporting people with learning disabilities should be pro-active in ensuring that the courts respond appropriately.

For the address of a local Law Centre, contact

The Law Centres Federation
Duchess House
18-19 Warren Street
London
N19 3NL

Tel   0171- 387 8570

Network for the Handicapped provides free specialist legal advice for people with physical and learning disabilities.

16 Princeton Street
London
WC1R 4BB

Tel   0171- 831 8031
or   0171- 831 7740

Most obvious is the need to check that the court is accessible for people with mobility disabilities – the majority are not. A court may have an induction loop, and must provide interpreters for deaf people or those who do not speak English as a first language. The court will probably accept assistance to understand someone with speech disabilities, if the 'interpreter' takes an oath, but this should be clarified before a hearing starts. Legal Aid may be available to pay for an interpreter.

Courts will usually arrange for cases concerning vulnerable witnesses to be heard promptly, if a request is made in advance. This is particularly important in a Magistrates' Court, where cases are often arranged for the convenience of solicitors not witnesses. Most courts will arrange waiting facilities which avoid the likelihood of the victim meeting the defendant, if asked.

Adjournment delays are still very common. In one instance a case concerning serious assaults had to be abandoned because the second hearing was delayed for a year, by which time one of the key witnesses was too ill to give evidence. **Courts might note that delays inevitably favour the defendant, especially if witnesses have learning disabilities.**

Preparation for court

The ideal way to become accustomed to courts is to visit as a member of the public *before the likelihood of personal involvement arises*. Courts are public buildings and, except in special circumstances, anyone can sit in the public gallery. Ushers will usually advise which cases are likely to be interesting. Groups can also use roleplay to develop their knowledge of court procedures (see Williams 1995).

If an individual is to appear in court, familiarization is now possible when the court is empty. It might be helpful for the witness to stand in the witness box, read the oath or affirmation, practise saying name, address and date of birth, answer questions asked from the lawyers' desks, and note where everyone will sit. If possible, it is important for a person with learning disabilities to practise in the same court-room in which they will appear. Courts vary greatly and it can be very distressing, for example, if the defendant appears where the victim thought the jury might be. This should be explained to the court clerk, when requesting a familiarization session.

Witnesses should never be coached on what to say in court. Defence lawyers commonly attempt to have cases concerning people with learning disabilities thrown out on this ground. However this does not mean that a victim-witness cannot be helped to understand the court process and prepare for basic questions.

If you are worried about appearing in court, we will show you a court-room before the case starts. You may then familiarise yourself with the layout...

Whenever possible you will be provided with a place to wait away from the other side involved in your court case.

Your family and friends may wish to be at the trial. We will help them and try to arrange seats for them in court. If possible this will be away from the other side involved in your court case.

The Courts Charter, Lord Chancellor's Department, 1992

Complaints in relation to the Courts Charter can be made to

The Court Service Secretariate
Lord Chancellor's Department
Trevelyan House
30 Great Peter Street
London SW1P 2BY

Tel   0171- 210 8832

The *Child Witness Pack* (NSPCC 1993) provides an excellent means to learn, for anyone – child or adult. Successful strategies have included: reducing anxiety, encouraging staff to respond to the victim's need to talk, building up self-esteem, expressing views about the perpetrator (Fraser 1993:7). If preparation is done formally, sessions might be videoed or recorded to demonstrate that this did not constitute coaching.

Perhaps the most important aspect of preparation is to make it clear that, if a case does not succeed, this does not mean that the victim-witness was lying or not believed or wrong; simply that the case was not proved. 'Not guilty' does not mean 'innocent'. It is helpful to remember that, one out of five of all Crown Court cases ends up with a 'not guilty' verdict.

It is useful to develop victim-witnesses' understanding of 'proof' because this may influence the way they then answer questions and the amount of detail they reveal. Juries and magistrates are often convinced of the truth of a person's evidence because of small, apparently irrelevant, detail which he or she could not otherwise have known, for example which hand was used for a particular action. Witnesses who may be confused about left and right, names of body parts, and descriptive vocabulary can be advised to demonstrate the things they saw.

Witnesses should be certain that they can say, **and recognize** their **full** name, with title (e.g. Miss Sonia Jasmin Jones), and their full address. If this might prove difficult, documentary evidence (birth certificate, NHS card, ID cards with photograph, etc) may be useful. The victim-witness can practice reading, or repeating in small sections, the oath or affirmation. Affirmations are very rarely used and the court usher or clerk should be advised in advance if the witness wishes this, not least because they may not be able to find a copy!

A witness with learning disabilities may be asked to explain the words 'oath', 'truth' and 'promise'. (Philosophers, for millennia, have kept themselves in employment arguing about the meaning of 'truth', but someone with learning disabilities is usually expected to supply a cogent definition in a sentence!) Easy definitions could be discussed, perhaps with examples:

> 'An oath is promising to tell the truth.'

> 'Telling the truth means saying what really happened – not making anything up, and not leaving anything out. If I say I went to the cinema on Monday that's true because I really went.'

> 'A promise is saying you will do something and doing it. Like saying you will to go to see a friend next Monday night, and going.'

A leaflet explaining court visits for people with learning disabilities, in Scotland, is available from

Crown Office Library
25 Chambers Street
Edinburgh
EH1 1LA

Tel   0131- 226 2626

I swear by Almighty God, that the evidence that I shall give shall be the truth, the whole truth and nothing but the truth.
Oath

I do solemnly, sincerely, and truly declare and affirm that the evidence I shall give shall be the truth, the whole truth and nothing but the truth.
Affirmation

Witnesses might also be introduced to obtuse court language – My Lord, adjourn, defendant, counsel, etc. They can also be reassured that it does not matter if they:

- cry
- stop
- ask to sit down
- ask for a drink of water
- ask to go to the toilet
- are asked to speak louder
- are asked to repeat things.

Witnesses can be told to:

- listen very carefully to questions
- say if they do not understand a question or cannot remember the answer
- correct something if they make a mistake or if someone misunderstands what they say
- say if they have not finished saying everything
- remember that the most important thing is to tell the court the truth.

Witnesses should know that they can correct anything a lawyer says or does that is wrong. A witness who says, 'No, not like that, with this [the left not right] arm' to a defending barrister who is demonstrating how someone had been hit, gains immediate credibility as a witness. Witnesses should also be warned that lawyers might

- ask 'tricky' and leading questions to catch them out
- say that they are lying
- get angry or rude
- be unpleasant, or a mixture of very nice and very aggressive
- tell a completely wrong story and try to get the witness to agree that it is true.

In Canada, the Ministry of the Attorney General (the counterpart of the CPS) accepts a direct responsibility for preparing children for court, and programmes are individually tailored to each victim-witness. **The CPS could usefully take on a greater responsibility for preparing vulnerable witnesses for court.**

Advice to lawyers

Prosecuting lawyers are not used to receiving advice about how to conduct cases, but many of the problems experienced by people with learning disabilities can be avoided if lawyers are made aware of a few basic points.

79

Memory is an obvious problem, and defence counsel will probably make a deliberate effort to discredit a vulnerable witness by pointing out inconsistencies in a statement to the police and evidence in the witness box. A simple strategy is to ask the witness to check his/her police statement just before the trial; simple, yet hardly ever thought of by prosecutors.

Reducing obvious sources of trauma can be straightforward. The use of screens to shield the victim from direct view of the accused and the removal of wigs and gowns has contributed to successful convictions. Many of the court preliminaries, such as swearing in the jury, can be done before the victim-witness enters court. Victim-witnesses might meet the judge and other court officers before a case. Measures should be taken to avoid unnecessary adjournments, for example independent psychological or psychiatric assessments might be obtained before a case is heard.

The court formality of addressing all witnesses as Mr X, Miss Y etc should be maintained for a witness with learning disabilities, and this should be suggested to the person's lawyers. If all other witnesses are addressed by title and surname, but one by a first name, this presents a childlike image of that person, which can create the impression that his or her evidence may be less reliable. Defending lawyers may use this as a deliberate tactic, which should be stopped by a judge or magistrates, or challenged by prosecuting counsel. Witnesses with learning disabilities should be made aware that they will be addressed formally (which may be the first time in their lives). Similarly, any use of 'girl' or 'boy' for an adult should be challenged.

Prosecution lawyers can be made aware of some of the tactics used by defence lawyers which (intentionally or not) have disconcerted vulnerable witnesses:

- repeating the same question many times
- pretending not to hear answers
- leaving very long silences
- temper tantrums such as throwing papers on the desk
- a sudden contrast of very gentle then very aggressive questioning
- congratulating witnesses on seeming 'cleverness'
- using a string of questions requiring a 'yes' answer, and then one crucial question requiring 'no'
- moving the victim into the centre of the court on the pretext of hearing answers better, but which also puts him/her close to the alleged attacker
- testing a witness on his/her ability to explain the difference between truth and falsehood – this should be the responsibility of the judge.

 A complaint against a solicitor should be addressed to

The Solicitor's Complaints Bureau
Portland House
Stag Place
London SW1

Tel   0171- 834 2288

 A complaint against a barrister can be made to

The General Council of the Bar
3 Bedford Row
London WC1

A judge has a responsibility to stop intimidation, and a formal objection to these forms of behaviour, even if over-ruled, alerts the judge that there may be a deliberate attempt to unnerve the witness. This is even more important in a magistrates' court where magistrates will have less confidence to challenge intimidation from lawyers. Expert witnesses can also be vulnerable and could benefit from reading *Professionals and the courts: a handbook for expert witnesses* (Carson 1990).

Reform

There is a clear need to improve court practice if the words of the Magna Carta, 'To no one deny or delay right of justice' are to have meaning for people with learning disabilities. The need is also evidenced by the trauma suffered by families supporting victim-witnesses through the courts. VOICE, an organization providing specialist support for families, reports that *most* cases end with the divorce of parents and in one instance a suicide. Specific innovations in other countries can indicate possible directions for progress.

Admissibility and the oath

In British courts, the judge must decide if a witness's evidence is *admissible:* can the person understand the meaning of truth and do they have the ability to tell the truth? The prevailing UK ethos is that it is for the person labelled as having intellectual disabilities to prove their competence (although in practice this may not always be the case). If appearing as a prosecution witness, the burden of proof of competence is put on the prosecution. In Canada changes to the Evidence Act 1988 place the burden of proof of incompetence on the party who challenges the mental capacity of the witness (Senn 1988: 67). There is no presumption that a person who is labelled as having an intellectual disability is incapable of giving evidence.

But even before a court has the chance to assess competence, a case can be blocked by the CPS on the basis of admissibility. Decisions concerning competence are often a guess by the CPS, based on another guess by a low-ranking police officer. A statement of IQ from the police, perhaps deriving from an assessment many years earlier when the victim was at school, could be the deciding factor. Yet, on the reliability of confession evidence by *suspects* with intellectual disabilities, appeal judges have ruled that 'the judicial approach to submissions...[should not] be governed by which side of an arbitrary line...the IQ fell', but by an independent psychological assessment (*Regina v Silcott et al*, 5 December 1991, reported in *The Times* 9 December 1991).

In the guise of ensuring the protection of persons with handicaps, but frequently more for the sake of the convenience and security of other persons, the law has traditionally concentrated on ways to establish formally the things that a person with a disability cannot do. All too often a person's perceived inability to do some things is translated by legal processes into a finding of inability to do anything. The law has not demonstrated much capacity to find ways in which the person's special needs can be accommodated so that he or she can participate in ordinary human activities, including the activity of doing justice in society.

O. Endicott, quoted in Bull 1994

81

Taking and understanding the oath is the first hurdle for people with learning disabilities, and arguably a completely redundant part of court procedure. Swearing to tell the truth is not a guarantee that someone will tell the truth, and an inability to take an oath or to explain what is meant by truth does not mean that an individual cannot or will not give a factual account of an event (Law Commission 1991: 40). A person may well understand the concept of truth, but not the language of the oath or the word truth. In Ireland the Criminal Evidence Act 1992 (s.27) now permits 'mentally handicapped' adults to give unsworn evidence, 'if the court is satisfied he [sic] is capable of giving an intelligible account of events which are relevant to those proceedings'.

An oath is not required for statements to the police, which are admitted as direct evidence. It is not required of children, or of witnesses giving evidence to parliamentary enquiries which are presided over by judges (MPs and Prime Ministers, for example, are apparently considered to be more honest than witnesses in court). Oath-taking might be replaced, for all witnesses, by a statutory warning that lying would have serious consequences.

The Australian Law Reform Commission has criticized the use of the oath as a test of competence (see Johnson, Andrew and Topp 1988: 66), proposing instead that:

1. A person who is incapable of understanding that, in giving evidence, he or she is under an obligation to give truthful evidence, is not competent to give evidence.

2. A person who is incapable of giving a rational reply to a question about a fact is not competent to give evidence about the fact.

This approach would mean that ways other than using an oath, for testing competence, might be used. Under recent changes to the Canada Evidence Act (as amended by Bill C-15, 1988), if a person cannot understand 'the nature of the oath or a solemn affirmation' he or she can testify 'on promising to tell the truth.' (Senn 1988: 67).

From observation in a busy magistrates' court it would be easy to conclude that there is a high correlation between religious belief and criminality – it is almost unknown for defendants to ask to take the affirmation instead of the religious oath. For a non-believer to swear on the Bible is akin to a promise with your fingers crossed, and this is obviously common practice. Muslim witnesses swear to a Christian God; people of polytheistic faiths swear to 'God' in the singular. Until recently Chinese witnesses took an oath which involved breaking a saucer – a practice which derived from the Imperial Courts many centuries ago, and is part of the initiation ritual of the Triads (JSB 1994: 2.9).

> Barrister:
> *In your life, have you ever told lies?*
>
> Witness:
> *Yes.*
>
> Does this indicate a witness who will tell the truth, or one who will not?

> Judge: *Do you understand what an oath is?*
> Mary: *No*
> Judge: *When you swear to tell the truth, will you tell the truth?*
> Mary: *(No answer)*
> Judge: *If you are asked to tell the truth, will you tell the truth?*
> Mary: *I don't know.*
> Judge: *Does an oath on a Bible bind you?*
> Mary: *(No answer)*
> Social worker:
> *Would it be all right if I help her out with the question?*
> Judge: *No it would not.*
> Prosecuting counsel:
> *My Lord, I wonder if the term 'bind you' would be understood by this lady?*
> Judge: *Do you believe in God?*
> Mary: *Could be yes, could be no.*
> Judge: *Let her be shown a Bible, please, usher. If you are asked to tell the truth today, will you tell the truth?*
> Mary: *Yes*
> Judge: *That book will make you tell the truth, will it?*
> Mary: *Yes.*

A case concerning a 20-year-old woman with learning disabilities, reported in the *Independent*, 29 November 1993: 15

Yet victims with learning disabilities can fail to achieve justice simply because they cannot, or choose not to, say an oath, or because they cannot lucidly explain the meaning of 'truth' - a test that is not applied to adults unless you bear the label of intellectual disability.

According to the Judicial Studies Board (JSB 1994: 2.3) a recent appeal ruling 'makes it clear that the only duty of a court is to consider whether the witness is taking an oath which appears to the court to be binding on the witness's conscience, and if so, whether it is an oath which the witness himself [sic] considers to be binding on his [sic] conscience.' From this ruling it is arguable that a person with learning disabilities could read a personal oath or affirmation, which is specially written in a style that the individual concerned understands, and that this would be lawful if both the court and the witness considered it to be binding.

Reliability

If the judge decides that a person's evidence is admissible, the jury must decide if evidence is *reliable*. It is, of course, as false to make generalizations about the reliability of people with learning disabilities as about any other social group. From the evidence provided by the press, it could well be concluded that, for example, international financiers are thoroughly unreliable when expected to tell the truth in court. Yet, at present, the judgement about the reliability of a witness with learning disabilities may well be based on little more than prejudice.

'Statement reliability analysis' has been proposed as a means to overcome the problem of prejudice. It has been used in Germany since 1954 (see Köhnken 1990). However German culture perhaps does not share the reservations, found in other countries, that 'mental disorder' cannot be labelled in a definitive way. What are the criteria for choosing who should have to undergo reliability analysis? If IQ is the determinate, many witnesses with apparent learning disabilities are likely to be borderline cases. Surely the decision that some individuals must undergo analysis is in itself an arbitrary pre-judgement likely to cast doubt on that person's reliability in court.

Canadian researchers, working on pilot programmes using 'statement validity analysis' with children, conclude that 'learning to apply it reliably takes significant training and practice' (Schroeder 1991: 16). How likely is it that relevant expertise could be available to every court in the country, without increasing the number of delays and intrusive expert interventions already suffered by witnesses? Under the Canada Evidence Act (as amended by Bill C-15, 1988), people with intellectual disabilities do not have to prove their capability – the burden of proof is on the person challenging.

Judges are increasingly helping juries to determine reliability by careful and informed summing up. In some instances they have commented before evidence is heard that, even if details (such as time, day and time sequence) are confused by a witness with intellectual disabilities, this is not necessarily an indication that the person is not relating an account of what happened in a factual manner. Such details are only important if they constitute direct evidence that could convict someone.

Communication

In some countries the concern about admissibility and reliability, in relation to witnesses with intellectual disabilities, is assuming less importance than removing communication barriers. Once communication problems are addressed, questions of admissibility and reliability are easier to resolve. For example recent revisions of the Canada Evidence Act (as amended by Bill C-15, 1988) change the 'sufficient intelligence' test to one of 'ability to communicate', and Section 6 provides for the possibility of non-verbal communication (Senn 1988: 67). A pragmatic discussion is provided by Ray Bull in 'Interviewing people with communicative disabilities' (1994).

In the UK, Legal Aid *may* be granted to pay for an interpreter for a witness with speech disabilities, but this is not certain. Under the Police and Criminal Evidence Act 1984 (PACE) an 'appropriate adult' is permitted to facilitate communication during a formal statement to the police in the case of someone who is detained or being questioned in police custody. But an 'appropriate adult' doing exactly the same in court can be seen as inappropriate. These inconsistencies can easily be addressed.

For witnesses with no speech 'facilitated communication' (the use of a keyboard with the help of a facilitator who supports the hand or arm) has been proposed, and opposed, as a viable means of giving evidence. The obvious concern is that the response may come from the facilitator rather than the person communicating. There have been cases of staff dismissal following allegations of sexual offences through facilitated communication, but the allegations have been strongly contested. In a case in Indiana, lawyers agreed a testing procedure for assessing the safety of facilitated evidence. The witness, a ten-year-old girl with severe learning disabilities and autism, was not, as a result, permitted to give evidence, but the acceptance of a procedure was itself a useful development (Bligh and Kupperman 1993). Facilitated communication opens more avenues for the initial reporting of victimization, but as yet, appears unsafe as a means of proving such allegations.

One unique development of police and court practice comes in the form of the *Protocol for Investigation and Prosecution of Cases Involving Persons with Special Communication Needs* of Nova Scotia (1991). 'Persons with special communication needs' are defined as, 'those individuals who, because of age, level of literacy, mental or physical disability are unable, without assistance, to fully access the criminal justice system or understand or be understood by officials thereof'. The protocol takes the emphasis away from disability, competence or reliability and places it on communication needs. It also does not make the mistake (common in UK policy) of viewing police, prosecution service and court practice in isolation from each other.

The Protocol provides that the police must arrange for a support person and interpreter, and for 'the use of special equipment or other assistance as required'. Interviews are to be video or audio-taped. The officer who commences the investigation must remain with the case to its conclusion.

The Nova Scotia prosecution service must then *assess* the witness's ability to communicate, and their understanding of the oath and of truth. This is done *before* the case reaches the courts. An assessment must be made of the victim's statement, and if it is inadequate the police or the prosecution service should re-interview. There is a responsibility to arrange for a thorough preparation of the witness for court, especially during the week preceding the case. The Crown Attorney must be assigned at the earliest opportunity and remain with the case until its conclusion.

The case must be heard at an early date; where appropriate the public may be excluded and the identity of the witness can be withheld. If the ability of the witness to testify is challenged the Crown must consider calling an expert witness to clarify the situation.

The Nova Scotia Protocol is an exemplary model which could be adopted in the UK, probably without law reform. It is not fundamentally at variance with existing UK procedures. The feature in greatest contrast to current British practice concerns any decision, by the prosecution service, not to prosecute. In Nova Scotia [emphasis added]:

> 'Prosecution of cases involving vulnerable witnesses **should be pursued wherever sufficient evidence exists** unless public interest considerations dictate otherwise. Where a decision is made not to prosecute, the reasons therefore **are to be discussed with the vulnerable witness** and, where appropriate the support person. Such discussion should be held **before the prosecution is stopped**. In addition, the reasons for stopping the prosecution are to be stated in the Crown file.'

Until very recently the *Code for Crown Prosecutors* in England did little more in respect of vulnerable witnesses than find excuses why cases should not proceed:

> 'The Crown Prosecutor...should have regard to the following matters...

> iii   Does it appear that a witness is exaggerating,.or that his memory is faulty, or that he...may be otherwise unreliable...

> vi   What sort of impression is the witness likely to make? How is he likely to stand up to cross-examination? Does he suffer from any physical or mental disability which is likely to affect his credibility?'

Thankfully, these conditions do not appear in the latest revision of the Code (CPS 1994), which instead lists under 'some common public interest factors in favour of prosecution': if 'the victim of the offence was vulnerable' (6.4, h); and if 'there is a marked difference between the actual or mental ages of the defendant and victim' (6.4, j).

If the CPS decides not to prosecute, the practice in the UK is to inform all parties of this decision without any prior discussion with the victim. The UK Code discourages re-starting a prosecution, and victims are therefore presented with a near irresible *fait accompli*, which would not happen in Nova Scotia. The main difference between the UK Code and the Nova Scotia Protocol is that the latter requires, rather than hopes for, good practice concerning vulnerable victims.

Regarding minor offences, which may be far from minor in the lives of victims with learning disabilities (see Chapter 3), the new CPS Code still discourages prosecution:

> '6.5   A prosecution is less likely to be needed if:
> a.   the court is likely to impose a very small or nominal penalty...
> b.   the offence was committed as a result of a genuine mistake or misunderstanding...
> c.   the loss or harm can be described as minor and was the result of a single incident, particularly if it was caused by a misjudgement'

The view of the state is now likely to be that overstaying the allotted time on a parking meter is more serious than locking a person in a room for fifteen minutes, shouting intimidating abuse relating to a person's disability, or opening someone's mail, because parking offences are automatically prosecuted.

At present a victim of a crime has no ultimate right to a police investigation of a report, of referral of a case to the CPS, or of prosecution. If the CPS proceed with a case, victim involvement is discretionary, and the court is under no obligation to hear any evidence from the victim.

In the criminal courts, the government is the ultimate gatekeeper to justice, and at present it seems to be a gatekeeper who is unsympathetic to vulnerable victims. In contrast, there is a right to a civil hearing, which is enshrined in the European Convention on Human Rights.

Video

There is considerable discussion about extending the use of TV links and video recorded interviews, already available for children, to vulnerable adults. There are precedents concerning adults. In May 1992 a witness in a UK court case gave evidence from the United States, via a live video link, in a civil case concerning negligence. Two months earlier video evidence had been given from Canada in a criminal case at the Old Bailey (Dyer 1992a: 4). A unique instance concerns a pensioner who recorded her testimony on video, including the examination-in-chief and cross-examination, because of a fear that she would be dead before the trial date (Dyer 1992b: 1).

There are no firm conclusions supporting the use of video links for children. In Canada the use of video links for child witnesses is reportedly now decreasing, as the proper preparation of witnessed has assumed a greater importance (Wade 1993: 24). One purpose of a video link is to reduce the 'injury' a court may cause to a witness, and thus to minimize the effect that 'injury' may have on the achievement of justice. Perhaps we should ultimately be reducing the source of the injury – the intimidating nature of courts and court practice (see Chapter 2) – rather than encouraging the sticking-plaster solution of video links. *All* victim-witnesses are vulnerable and *no one* should be further victimized by courts. Where a video is the only possible means of representation in court, precedents seem to exist for its use.

Should people with learning disabilities have a special legal status in court?

There is current debate about the benefits of according victims with learning disabilities a special legal status in court. At first this might seem an appealing solution to the disabilities they experience, in part because reform could mirror that for children. However there are many arguments against a special status, not least that it goes against all principles of 'ordinary living' and non-discrimination.

A key problem is the definition of 'learning disabilities'. All definitions are arbitrary. Current legal definitions (eg 'mental defective') only concern those with profound, indisputable disabilities. Whilst more general, needs-based definitions are pragmatically applied for the provision of services, it would be very difficult to construct a clear, general definition for court purposes, especially concerning borderline cases. In 1973,

87

in the USA, a formal definition was changed very slightly by one standard deviation, with the result that 8 million people were, overnight, not 'retarded'. It is those people who are on the borderlines of formal definitions who are most likely to appear as victim-witnesses, and often they have never been formally assessed.

Recent research for the New South Wales Law Reform Commission (Australia) included the remit to determine 'whether there should be a new uniform statutory definition of 'intellectual disability'' (Hayes 1993:v), yet this was not achieved. A recent report from the Royal Commission on Criminal Justice (Gudjonsson, Clare, Rutter and Pearse 1993), called 'The identification of vulnerabilities' recommended, '...what is urgently needed is an operational definition of mental disorder and vulnerability' (p.27), but the report failed to suggest how this might be done.

One of the strongest arguments against giving 'learning disabilities' legal meaning, is that it could set unforeseen precedents, which might be to the detriment of people with learning disabilities, as has happened in other circumstances. For example, Poll Tax legislation caused considerable concern that those claiming exemption because of 'mental impairment' might then lose rights under the Mental Health Act and the right to vote.

There are also persuasive arguments against stereotyping on the basis of formal assessments, such as IQ testing. For example, two people with the same IQ rating may have very varying memories and ideas of truthfulness – just like the general populace. It is also claimed that the IQ score of an individual with learning disabilities can be improved by 20–25 points with a few weeks training (Williams 1993a: 24), and so a legal definition based on a difference of one point would be a nonsense. IQ testing becomes very unreliable when a learning disability is combined with other disabilities, particularly sensory ones, which is common. The New South Wales report (mentioned above) points out that any form of assessment is based largely on IQ testing, and cites American work which concluded, '...the ability to distinguish right from wrong...to be a witness...depends on many factors among which intelligence is only one' (p.6). It is worth considering that the competence of victim-witnesses has already been demonstrated before cases reach the CPS, by their ability or not to make a formal statement to the police.

It is similarly questionable to try to assess memory *per se*, as memory can depend on what type of event an individual is trying to recall. Research shows that, whilst many adults can remember well incidents in childhood that are related to mild trauma (such as moving house), the level of accuracy when recalling recent routine events (such as the use of a cash-card) is very low. Some people may find it easier to recall events that relate to someone else (e.g. an assault on friend) than events relating to themselves (e.g. personal assault), but for others the reverse may be true.

The capabilities of a witness with learning disabilities are also affected by how questions are asked. Recent work about police interviewing techniques and people with learning disabilities addresses this point (Bull and Cullen 1992). The influence of the questioner was demonstrated very lucidly by the reply of the sister of a woman with learning disabilities, who was giving evidence at an inquest. When asked by the coroner if the woman could understand and answer basic questions the sister replied simply that 'It depended on who was asking the questions.'

Lawyers sometimes appear to take advantage of witness vulnerabilities (see Chapter 2). Observed techniques include: needlessly repeating the same question, pretending not to hear answers, moving a witness closer to the accused on the pretext of the court hearing replies better, congratulating witnesses on using long words. This again demonstrates that vulnerability can have more to do with the context of the court than with an individual's personal abilities.

Standard assessments relating to learning disabilities are also culturally biased (Ward, in Williams 1993a: 52). Their use in court proceedings concerning victims from black and minority ethnic groups would be politically sensitive and could lead to challenges.

Most importantly, if the definitions used are not acceptable to the witnesses concerned, their rejection will frustrate rather than promote justice. Unlike the implementation of definitions concerning 'mentally disordered' offenders, the justice system requires the co-operation of victim-witnesses, which means that practice must be 'politically correct'. In North America it is now quite common for people with learning disabilities to refuse to undertake any form of testing or assessment.

6
CHAPTER

Alternatives to the criminal system

Civil action

Civil cases are proven on a less strict standard (the 'balance of probabilities') than in the criminal court ('beyond reasonable doubt'). Rules of evidence are also different. Therefore, if there are witnesses with learning disabilities a civil case may be more appropriate. Someone with learning disabilities can sue through someone else, a 'next friend', (RSC ord 80, CCR ord 10 and pt IX of the Family Proceedings Rules 1991). For claims of over £1000, it is usual to use a lawyer. Legal aid is available (or not) in the usual way.

A number of recent civil cases, setting new precedents, are particularly relevant to the lives of people with learning disabilities. The first raises the possibility of suing a service provider for not protecting a service user from bullying. An action has been started against a Scottish school by a woman who claims that her exam results, and therefore career, were affected because of bullying (Renton 1993: 11). Of more relevance, in England a woman with cerebral palsy (now a law student) sued her school because teachers did not protect her from 'disablist' bullying (Ward 1994: 2). The outcome was unsuccessful, but, as the woman's father said, 'a point has been made.' There will inevitably be a deterrent effect.

A civil case may also be pursued, if a criminal case fails on a technicality. A man who was cleared of murdering a young girl, on the grounds of 'oppressive questioning' by the police, was then sued for 'battery on the child X resulting in her death' (*Independent* 19 May 1994: 5).

Another use of civil law concerns defamation, which is frequently suffered by vulnerable people, yet damages claims are rarely considered. It is even possible to sue for 'slander by conduct' if the reputation of an individual is harmed by a degrading act in public. Unreasonable, humiliating, public arrest by a police officer might fall into this category.

Bringing a defamation case may be particularly relevant if a resident has been accused verbally of a sexual assault (perhaps by a staff member on the information of another resident) but no evidence is available to substantiate the assault claim. The usual difficulty in such cases, having to establish that an individual's reputation has been damaged by the slander, does not apply if the allegation is of an imprisonable offence (such as sexual or common assault). The main difficulty with such defamation cases would, however, remain – legal aid is not available. However, the realization by staff that the law supports, at least in theory, that unsubstantiated allegations against *anyone* are unacceptable is important.

The small claims court (information about which is available from the local County Court) deals with claims for damages for under £1000. Each party must pay their own costs irrespective of who wins. Hearings are usually in an office setting, not a court. Lawyers are discouraged and those hearing cases are experienced at assisting people who may be unused to court practice. However, before embarking on any attempt to obtain financial damages, consider if the perpetrator can pay. Although a court may direct payments by weekly instalments, the order will not usually be for more than one year. It is proposed that, in the future, the small claims court will also deal with minor cases concerning personal injury.

Finally, it may be possible to get an injunction under civil proceedings if it is feared that a person may suffer from assault of harassment, nuisance, false imprisonment, trespass. This might be used to obtain an assurance that a particular act will not happen while a case is waiting to come to court, for example that staff will not continue to lock residents in rooms.

Staff disciplinary proceedings

Disciplinary proceedings should not be an alternative to reporting to the police. They may parallel a police investigation, or be considered if the police or CPS can take no further action following a report. There are a number of advantages and disadvantages to consider before determining an appropriate strategy in relation to disciplinary proceedings.

The principal advantage of disciplinary proceedings is that the burden of proof is not as high as in a criminal or civil case. 'Reasonable grounds' to believe that an offence, relevant to an employees position, was committed is sufficient for dismissal. Even if an employee is acquitted by a court, dismissal may still be lawful.

Employers do not have to wait for the outcome of a court case before dismissing someone who has apparently broken the law. Even if an employee was dismissed following proceedings that were not technically in accord with the ACAS (Advisory, Conciliation and Arbitration Service) Code of Practice, the dismissal may still be lawful.

Disabled boy forces Sun to pay for 'worst brat' libel

The six-year-old boy who was branded the 'worst brat in Britain' by the Sun won substantial libel damages yesterday and made legal history by becoming the first child in the UK to sue for defamation.

...the article alleged that J had wrecked his parent's home, cut off his own ear, and killed the family cat in the washing machine.
It also said he had twice set fire to living room furniture and flooded the bathroom by ripping pipes from the wall. It added that J had painted the dog with blue emulsion paint, smashed two video recorders and swallowed insecticide... 'Unfortunately at the time the article was published the editor and staff of the Sun were unaware that J was registered disabled, that he contacted acute neonatal meningitis at birth, and that he suffers from Attention Deficit Hyperactivity Disorder which causes behavioural problems'. 'As J's disability was not mentioned in the article, it left the impression that he was wilfully naughty and his mother had brought him up to be so.'

The Guardian, 24 May 1991: 3

If a man is dismissed for stealing, as long as the employer honestly believes it on reasonable grounds, that is enough to justify dismissal. It is not necessary for the employer to prove that he was in fact stealing

Lord Denning

Possible offences that relate to the trust embodied in an employment position can be taken especially seriously. Assault and sexual offences would be clear grounds for dismissing someone with a duty to care. (For general information about disciplinary proceedings see Pritchard 1992: 469).

Informal resolutions before a formal hearing are also possible. The defendant might be shown video or taped evidence from the victims or witnesses, which might precipitate a voluntary resignation or transfer request.

It is not important to what level or degree an employee may have offended, simply that an offence, which could relate to the job a person is expected to do, may have been committed. An employee can be dismissed for hitting someone once – there does not have to be a proven pattern of repeated assaults.

Action is often taken on the basis of everything that is alleged. Instead, managers might consider pursuing one or two incidents, which are easy to prove and which clearly constitute offences. (The CPS takes the same approach.) It could be agreed with all parties, before a hearing, that one offence is sufficient to warrant dismissal. If a case is not successful on the grounds of a particular alleged offence, new hearings can be pursued based on other allegations. But if a 'package' of allegations is dismissed, second chances are almost impossible. It is much easier for an accused person to frustrate and prolong more complex proceedings. There is more room for side-tracking, stopping a hearing on the grounds of technicalities, and discrediting witnesses. If doubt is cast on a witness because of a memory lapse concerning a peripheral incident, this could jeopardize a whole case.

In disciplinary proceedings, the people defending (often union representatives) are concerned principally with preserving an employee's job, not with establishing the truth or achieving justice for a vulnerable person. They are likely to welcome, and even precipitate, anything that will lead to a hearing being abandoned. Their tactics can include:

> 'talking out' the time allotted to the hearing so that further hearings are necessary

> causing an adjournment on a (perhaps incorrect) technicality. Unlike courts, those presiding over disciplinary proceedings sometimes cannot give immediate rulings on procedure or law

> reminding witnesses, who may be in the same union as the union representative and defendant, of union 'solidarity'

> asking for a rehearing on the grounds of a technicality, which may entail staff and people with learning disabilities repeating their stories.

Another problem is that appeals may be heard by people who have no knowledge of learning disabilities, the law, how to run an appeal, or how to maintain an unbiased 'judicial mind' – city councillors, for example. Witnesses have had their evidence doubted because hitting adults with learning disabilities is seen as being no different to smacking a naughty child; because it is not realized that any 'corrective' physical or verbal strategies by staff cannot be justified if the subject has no understanding of the link between the undesired action and the related punishment; or on the basis that the witness is homosexual and therefore 'over-sensitive' to acts by a staff member that amount to assaults.

Staff disciplinary proceedings were originally intended for disputes in industrial settings. The process does not envisage victims who may be especially vulnerable, nor situations where there is a professional caring relationship. In industrial settings, managers and shop-floor workers usually belong to different unions. In care settings managers and workers often belong to the same union, which creates a conflict of loyalties for union representatives defending individuals.

The most worrying aspect of disciplinary proceedings is that a staff member who is dismissed for, say, sexual assault, can still very easily obtain similar employment elsewhere in the country. However, the outcome of proceedings can be communicated, factually, to professional bodies such as the Royal College of Nursing, which may then withdraw the individual's membership. There seems no reason why any organization, statutory or voluntary, could not keep a list of staff who have been dismissed and make factual information available nationally to potential employers.

Social/Health Services complaints procedures

Complaints procedures should rarely be used in relation to allegations of crime. Usually, if a complaints officer finds that a complaint involves a possible offence the procedure will be suspended and the police informed. The main use of complaints in relation to victimization, is to redress a failure of duty to care, which would otherwise require costly civil action, and which may not, as the law stands at present, constitute a clear offence.

Complaints procedures might be used to establish facts, which may later constitute evidence for a criminal or civil case, for example, when evidence may be buried in case notes and other files, or witnesses are not immediately identifiable to the complainant. In such circumstances the police might feel initially that the probable offences were too minor to justify their time investigating, but might take up a case once the facts were more clearly established.

If a complaint against a Health Service is not dealt with properly, contact

The Health Service Ombudsman
Church House
Great Smith Street
London SW1P 3BW

Tel   0171-276 3000

or, for complaints against Social Services

The Local Government Ombudsman (The Commission for Local Administration in England): address from the local Citizen's Advice Bureau

Criminal Injuries Compensation Board (CICB)

Compensation can be claimed, whether or not a case goes to court, for an injury caused by a 'violent' criminal offence. Claims are not accepted for sums under £1000, and the police must have been informed 'without delay' (but not necessarily immediately following the injury). Victim Support (see local phone book) can help with claims.

The sum awarded by the CICB will equate with that which a court might award. As a guide, the following are around the £1000 threshold:

- Minor injury causing 2–3 weeks' absence from work £550–£850

- Fractured little finger; assuming full recovery after a few weeks £750

- Sprain, depending on loss of mobility £100–£1000

- Facial scar, however small resulting in permanent disfigurement £750+

- Loss of a front tooth £1000

- Nasal – displaced fracture of bone requiring manipulation £1000

- Wrist – simple fracture with complete recovery in few weeks £1750–£2500

- Fractured jaw (wired) – £2750

    (Magistrates' Association – *Sentencing Guidelines* 1993)

Any compensation paid by the CICB may be deducted from the victim's Income Support. Victims A and B may receive identical compensation for identical injuries. Victim B ends up with less cash because she receives Income Support. Victim A has nothing deducted from his £4k p.a. salary. If in addition victim A receives compensation via insurance (and individuals who are employed are more likely to have personal injury insurance), he may avoid declaring this, but the CICB will automatically arrange for the deduction from victim B's benefits. Most people with disabilities will be in the B category; the system clearly discriminates against people with learning disabilities as a group.

The official Department of Social Security view is that this deduction is reasonable because 'an injured person should not have the same need met twice' (private correspondence

August 1993). But Income Support is not intended to meet the needs generated by an injury. State benefits are calculated to permit an individual to lead a modest but normal life. Injury from violent crime is not an envisaged part of this life. This is recognised for those with jobs, but not for those without. **It is unreasonable for the state to deduct CICB compensation from state benefits that are unrelated to the injury in question.**

Domestic victimization

If there is 'a serious risk to the life, health or well-being of the residents' in a Registered Home, it may be closed down 'urgently' by an application to a single magistrate (see R. Jones 1993: 32). Any person with reasonable grounds for concern could contact the clerk at the local magistrates' court (usually day or night), ask the police to find a magistrate, or ask a magistrate directly. In the latter case the magistrate is unlikely to act without advice from the court clerk. Alternatively, if the matter is not urgent, an investigation can be carried out by a Registered Homes Tribunal (see Ashton and Ward 1992: 360). The local Social Services department or an MP could instigate such an investigation.

The National Assistance Act 1948 is another protective measure. On the advice of two doctors, a magistrate could order the removal of a person from a place of residence in relation to offences of 'act' or 'omission'. This can be done very quickly, and may, in some circumstances be useful when offences are being committed between people with learning disabilities in a group home (see R. Jones 1993: 33).

Guardianship under the Mental Health Act 1983 provides another route for protecting the welfare of a person, who is technically a 'patient', to a safe environment. The application must be supported by two doctors and made to the local social services department by an approved social worker or by the patient's nearest relative (see Ashton and Ward 1992: 196). This course of action may not be in the best interests of victims as it can be restrictive of their freedom.

Invoking an inspection is another power within the Mental Health Act (s115). An approved social worker may enter and inspect any place where a 'patient' is living (except a hospital), if they have grounds for believing that there is a lack of care. Forcible entry is not permitted but it would be an offence to prevent such an inspection.

The Law Commission proposed in 1993 that social workers should have powers to enter the homes of people they believe to be incapacitated and at risk. Social service departments would have such a duty. This followed the case of Beverly Lewis, a deaf and blind woman with learning disabilities who, in 1989, died of pneumonia, in squalor. Although social workers

A person may be removed from a place of residence if

(ii)   the person is unable to devote to himself, and is not receiving from other persons, proper care and attention; and

(iii)   his removal is necessary, either in his own interests or for preventing injury to the health of, or serious nuisance to, other persons

National Assistance Act 1948 s.47; National Assistance (Amendment) Act 1951 s.1.

knew that her mother, who suffered from schizophrenia, was not taking proper care of her daughter, they felt unable to act. The proposal is questioned by some carers associations who feel that it would lead to intrusive practice.

Inquests

When the circumstances of the death of a person with learning disabilities are related to a perceived failure of duty to care, an inquest might provide a verdict that can form the basis for criminal or civil action. It can also force the disclosure of facts that can be used to make a formal complaint, and make the public and service providers aware of important shortcomings.

At an inquest of a family where the parents had taken their own lives and that of their daughter there was evidence of bad practice within health and social services, and letters and notes from the family linking their dissatisfaction with their suicide. The verdict could not embrace failure of duty to care, because this was not clearly a direct cause. In another case, where a man had choked to death eating sandwiches, such a verdict was possible. In both cases the families were insistent that an inquest should be held, but had to pay their own costs. **Legal Aid should be made available to individuals who require representation at an inquest, if there is a public interest concern because of implications for public services.**

Health and Safety regulations

Health and Safety regulations provide another route for ensuring that responsible agencies note their failings, whether in residential or other service settings. After a boy with epilepsy drowned in a school swimming pool, the school was fined £4500 for failing to assess properly the risks associated with his epilepsy. The school had disregarded an instruction that a parent should always be present at swimming lessons, and there had been no head count after the lesson. The young man was only missed at the end of the school day when his mother called to ask where he was.

The advantage of using Health and Safety regulations is that the local authority's environmental heath department will pursue investigations and take a case through the courts, if appropriate, without cost or inconvenience to the victim or family.

For advice about health and safety contact environmental health departments of the local authority or the Health and Safety Executive in the local phone book.

People First scores landmark victory in
Ontario Court of Appeal

People First of Ontario has been involved for nearly a year in inquests called to investigate the deaths of 19 children and adults in two institutions... It appeared that the deaths of the children...involved the use of morphine in frequent very large doses in place of drugs and other interventions... The children also had 'Do not resuscitate' orders written on their charts...the apparent common cause of death was regurgitation and inhalation of food, leading to lung damage and asphyxiation...

People First applied to the court for Judicial Review of the coroners' decision to withhold the records, halting both inquests... The Divisional Court ruled against People First... People First then went to the Ontario Court of Appeal...and the Appeal Court reversed the Divisional Court ruling... The Appeal Court ordered that the records be delivered to People First. That organisation has since brought to light evidence of what was glaringly wrong with the medical care the deceased children were receiving... When the jury delivered its recommendations...they included many points that People First raised, especially that people with severe disabilities should never be discriminated against by withholding life-sustaining medical care.

Orville Endicott, *Entourage*, vol 7 no.1 1992

Mediation

There are voluntary mediation projects in many areas, which may be able to advise on staff training about conflict resolution, and provide a mediator in some circumstances. The decision to use mediation should entail an assessment that the relative power of the parties concerned is about equal. For example, mediation might be appropriate between two male service users, but not between a man and a younger woman and almost certainly not between a service user and a member of staff. There is usually an agreement by both parties that they will accept the decision given.

In the absence of mediation projects, day centres might consider using people from the community who have mediation or judicial skills (industrial arbitrators, magistrates, court officials, solicitors). But it should be made clear that these individuals are not acting in an official capacity. If day centres set up mediation committees, everyone must know that this does not have the power of a court or the police. Punishments (as distinct from agreeing reparation) must never be imposed by committees or staff, because this would probably be unlawful.

European and international rights

European law now takes precedence over UK law – European law *is* UK law. European human rights guarantees can be used to change British common law (Dyer 1992c: 4), but it would still be hard to find a police officer who would accept this point as an argument for pursuing a prosecution. The Crown Prosecution Service, however, is likely to take account of arguments based on European law, but would probably need to be reminded to do so.

The European Court usually takes six or seven years to reach a verdict. However, an outline knowledge of European law is useful because the threat of taking a case to Europe can be very effective. Britain has attracted more judgements against its government than any other nation, and Ministers are sensitive about this fact. The CPS will certainly take notice if they believe a case may go to Europe, so it is sometimes worth backing up a formal complaint with the relevant European statute. The European Convention on Human Rights (1953) is remarkably relevant to the lives of people with learning disabilities.

An awareness of European and international human rights law should influence all decisions concerning the achievement of justice for people with learning disabilities. The possibility of appeals to the European court, if appropriate, should be indicated in all relevant discussions.

 For further information:

MEDIATION UK
82a Gloucester Road
Bishopston
Bristol BS7 8BN

Forum for Initiatives in Reparation and Mediation (FIRM)
19 London End
Beaconsfield
Bucks
HP9 2HN

Alan Steer
(specifically concerning people with learning disabilities)
The City Literary Institute
16 Stukeley Street
Off Drury Lane
London
WC2B 5LJ

 Copies of the Convention and a brief guide to its implementation can be obtained from

European Commission of Human Rights
Council of Europe
BP 431 R6
67006 Strasbourg Cédex
France.

 Organisations such as *Liberty* may help to take cases to Europe.

Liberty
21 Tabard Street
London
SE1

Tel   0171-403 3888

The European Convention on Human Rights in relation to people with learning disabilities

The enjoyment of the rights and freedoms set forth in this Convention shall be secured without discrimination on any ground... (Art. 14)

Everyone's right to life shall be protected by law. (Art. 2)

No one shall be subjected to torture or to inhuman or degrading treatment or punishment. (Art. 3)

No one shall be required to perform forced or compulsory labour. (Art. 4,2)

Everyone has the right to liberty and security of person. (Art. 5,1)

Everyone who is arrested shall be informed promptly, in a language which he understands, of the reasons for his arrest and of any charge against him. (Art. 5,2)

 Everyone who has been the victim of arrest or detention in contravention of the provisions of this Article shall have an enforceable right to compensation. (Art. 5,5)

Everyone charged with a criminal offence has [the right] to have free assistance of an interpreter if he cannot understand or speak the language used in court. (Art. 6,3e)

Everyone has the right to respect for his private and family life, his home and his correspondence. (Art. 8,1)

There shall be no interference by a public authority with the exercise of this right except such as in accordance with the law... (Art. 8,2)

Everyone has the right to freedom of thought, conscience and religion...and in public or private, to manifest his religion or belief, in worship, teaching, practice and observance. (Art. 9,1.)

Everyone has the right to freedom of expression. This right shall include freedom to hold opinions and to receive and impart information and ideas without interference by public authority... (Art. 10,1)

Everyone has the right to freedom of peaceful assembly and to freedom of association with others... (Art. 11,1)

No restrictions shall be placed on the exercise of these rights other than such as are prescribed by law... (Art. 11,2)

Men and women of marriageable age have the right to marry and to found a family... (Art. 12)

Everyone whose rights and freedoms as set forth in this Convention are violated shall have an effective remedy before a national authority notwithstanding that the violation has been committed by persons acting in an official capacity. (Art. 13).

Every...person is entitled to the peaceful enjoyment of his possessions. No one shall be deprived of his possessions... (First Protocol Art. 1)

No person shall be denied the right to education... In the exercise of any functions which it assumes in relation to education and to teaching, the State shall respect the right of parents to ensure such education and teaching in conformity with their own religious and philosophical convictions. (First Protocol, Art. 2)

Everyone...shall have the right to liberty of movement and freedom to choose his residence. (Fourth Protocol, Art. 2, 1)

Everyone shall be free to leave any country, including his own. (Art. 2,2)

A case can only be brought to the European Court if all national remedies have been exhausted. This usually means that a final appeal to the House of Lords has failed. However, if a case was blocked by the Crown Prosecution Service, apparently without good reason, there may be two options. First, if an 'act' or 'omission' appeared to be against European law, but the CPS concluded that it was not against national law, this may provide grounds for a direct appeal to Europe. Second, Article 13, which states that there must be an effective national remedy for violations of the Convention, might be used either to pursuade the CPS to prosecute or as grounds for petitioning Europe.

Another code, which may assist in arguments for justice, is the International Covenant on Civil and Political Rights 1966 (ICCPR). The UK government has agreed to be bound by this (see Liberty 1993). Much of the ICCPR is similar to the European Convention, but it puts more emphasis on non-discrimination. The rights contained in the ICCPR must be upheld 'without distinction of any kind', and to comply with Article 14 the Government must ensure that people with 'mental disorder' have equal access to the courts and other hearings.

International Covenant on Civil and Political Rights 1966

Everyone shall have the right to recognition everywhere as a person before the Law (Art. 16)

All persons are equal before the law and are entitled without any discrimination to the equal protection of the law... (Art. 26)

States...[shall] ensure the equal right of men and women to the enjoyment of all civil and political rights set forth in the present Covenant. (Art. 3)

...no one shall be subjected without his free consent to medical or scientific experimentation. (Art. 7)

No one shall be subjected to arbitrary or unlawful interference with his privacy, family, home or correspondence, nor to unlawful attacks on his honour and reputation. (Art. 17,1)

Everyone has the right to the protection of the law against such inteference or attacks. (Art. 17,2)

Every citizen shall have the right and the opportunity, without any [distinction of any kind] and without reasonable restrictions... to vote (Art. 25,5)

Every citizen shall have the right and the opportunity...To have access, on general terms of equality, to public service in their country. (Art. 25(c))

7

CHAPTER

Invisible victims?

Invisible

out of sight..unseen..
unrecognised..poorly defined..
unnoticed..concealed..confused..
secret..imperceptible..hidden..
unapparent

Roget's Thesaurus 1987

people *out of sight*

People with learning disabilities and the circumstances that surround their lives have, for centuries, been kept out of sight. We may now be closing the unseen 'back-wards' of the mental handicap hospitals, but community care has yet to create lifestyles that are truly ordinary – lifestyles that are noticed. People do not have a statutory right to be known.

Rarely are people with learning disabilities the statistical one-in-thirty-three that they should be in every bus, theatre audience, or restaurant. They are certainly not three per cent of those who make complaints to the police or who receive compensation for crime. Whether victims or not, people with learning disabilities are not fully visible to the community.

unseen barriers to justice

But, of course, victims with learning disabilities are not 'invisible'. At the very least they are known to their victimizers, and probably to family, friends and professionals. It is the *barriers* between the victims and redress that are unseen thus *creating* the invisibility of the victims.

It is not just that any particular barrier blocks the path to justice. It is that in combination they constitute an insurmountable hurdle. The purpose of this chapter is to remind that these individual barriers remain largely unrecognized, but also to show that, as a totality, they make justice elusive.

unseen as victims

The greatest single barrier is in our minds – the stereotyped view of people with learning disabilities. They have always been seen more readily as potential offenders than as potential victims. A man who has suffered considerable racial abuse comments perceptively,

> 'At special school I was taught not to pinch other children's sweets and money. I was not taught, if I am in trouble, to tell the police.'

The academic literature abounds with books and papers about offenders; there are a handful of publications about victimization. Government committees produce copious reports about 'mentally disordered offenders', and nothing about victims. Whilst the Mental Health Act 1983 is often used to remove individuals from a public place 'for the protection of other persons' (s.136 (1)), the same Act is rarely considered as a means to remove someone who 'is being ill-treated' to safety (s.135 (1)).

Case law on defamation establishes that to allege that someone has an undesirable intellectual condition provides grounds for a claim for damages. The same holds for an unsubstantiated allegation that someone has committed an offence – impugning criminality or intellectual problems is regarded, in law, as synonymous and equally damaging to an individual's reputation. In addition, whilst there are countless examples of defamation of adults with learning disabilities, through unsubstantiated allegations that they have committed offences, there are no examples of damages awards through the courts.

Redressing the stereotyped view of people with learning disabilities, in relation to crime, is the key step in improving the current situation.

unrecognized crimes

Recognition of crime is the starting point for achieving redress, yet people with learning disabilities are rarely taught to conceptualize crime from the perspective of victims. People's perception can become further blurred if they are constantly taught to tolerate victimization. A learning difficulty is imposed on a learning disability.

This situation is compounded because professionals also do not recognize crime – when the victims are service users. Members of day centres commonly suffer assaults from other members and sometimes from staff, yet managers react in surprise to the suggestion of police involvement. Criminal assaults that would attract compensation of over a hundred pounds in a court, attract no more than a dab of Dettol if they happen in a day centre.

'False imprisonment' is common against people with learning disabilities. Being locked in a room or even told to stay there under threat, is unlawful. Technically the offence is indictable, yet members of the legal profession will confirm that it is very unusual for the police to bring charges for victims with or without learning disabilities. Why? 'False imprisonment' is rarely suffered by the general populace, and if it is, remedy is usually sought through the civil courts. The criminal route, which is usually most appropriate for people with learning disabilities, is rarely used and therefore rarely considered.

Talk to any group of people with learning disabilities about the bad things that happen to them and very soon they will tell of being frightened by harassment, verbal abuse or insults in the streets. The incidents they report are often clearly Public Order offences, yet there is not one example of a report resulting in a court case. Staff and parents are well aware that these things happen, the police are sometimes told, but insults are simply seen as something that people with learning disabilities must learn to tolerate.

Because the social environment of people with learning disabilities is largely other people with learning disabilities, victims are usually surrounded by witnesses who also may not recognize crime. Even if victims understand when to report, finding someone to corroborate the report is significantly more difficult than for those surrounded by people who can conceptualize crime clearly.

unrecognized perpetrators

Perpetrators are not recognized as perpetrators. Care professionals are viewed as beyond reproach. Families are seen as providing dutiful care and safe environments. The pinching, punching and pushing suffered by service users in service settings is never viewed as crime, because the offenders have learning disabilities. Children are significant perpetrators, yet verbal intimidation, petty assaults or thrown missiles are rarely responded to as criminal acts. In the stories related by people with learning disabilities, the police sometimes feature as victimizers. There have been headline reports of wrongful arrest and improper prosecution. But stories of people being picked up by police through incorrect use of the Mental Health Act 1983 (s. 136) go unreported.

103

Victimization by organizations, particularly, Health or Social Services, can be insidious and pervasive in the lives of service users. Even failures of duty leading to deaths are usually seen as management problems not criminal acts. It is possible to prosecute an organization, but virtually unheard-of, and community care legislation does not embody a duty to care. Those of us who do not rely on public services are usually ignorant of organizational victimization, so it remains largely unnoticed.

These are the significant perpetrator groups – staff, families, people with learning disabilities, children, police, and organizations. But they do not readily match our ideas of 'criminals', and this greatly hinders detection and redress.

poorly defined laws

Does the law clearly help victims to achieve redress? Very often not, because legislation made before community care does not take account of the new lifestyles of people with learning disabilities. The Sexual Offences Act (1956 s. 21 (1)) concerning abduction, for example, assumes that all people with learning disabilities are in 'the possession' of a guardian from whom they are abducted. Thus it excludes anyone living independently. The Act does not include men and omits the possibility of abduction for sexual offences between women. Both these circumstances could relate to vulnerable people.

Similarly, whilst the Mental Health Act 1959 makes it unlawful for a man to have sexual intercourse with a female patient, sexual offences by women and between men are ignored. The Sexual Offences Act 1956 (s. 27 (1)) can deter managers reporting because there appears to be a duty put on them to prevent sexual assaults on service users. This may be a reasonable duty in a hospital setting, but less so in a group home and certainly not for managers of independent living schemes.

The legal status of group homes poses other problems – a building that is home to some and workplace to others. Not least, traditionally the police are reluctant to interfere in domestic victimization. These attitudes have yet to change in recognition of the nature of group homes, which are only partly domestic.

Consenting homosexual acts, between people with learning disabilities, in the bedroom of a group home might be illegal because they are not technically done 'in private' (Sexual Offences Act 1967 (s.1. (1)). But indecent exposure by a staff member to a resident in the same bedroom may not be illegal because it was not done in 'a public place'. Police use the Mental Health Act 1983 (s.136 (1)) to remove people from group homes who threaten others. In this circumstance a group home becomes a 'public place'.

The Public Order Act 1986 appears problematic because it does not relate to acts in a 'dwelling', but there is no clarification relating to the semi-public areas of group homes. It could be a Public Order offence for a member of staff to shout, 'Come here you cretin I'm going to thump you' if this was done in a garden shed. But it is not clear if a Public Order offence would be committed if the setting were a staff room or any of the other semi-public areas which exist in many group homes. The Act does, of course, *not* pose a practical problem, because in its present unclear form no one thinks to use it in relation to service settings.

The Public Order Act 1986 (s.18 (1)) also deals with intent to stir up of racial hatred. But there is no legislation dealing with, what is increasing called, 'disablist' hatred. The skinhead who says to his friends, as a black man walks past,

> 'Let's go and sort out that black monkey. We don't want people from the jungle round here.'

probably commits a Public Order offence attracting severe punishments because of the racial element. If instead he choses to say, as someone with learning disabilities goes by,

> 'Let's go and sort out that imbecile. We don't want people from the looney bin round here.'

the law does not give the same weight to the offence. Germany provides an omen, historically and currently, of how circumstances can evolve if disablist hatred goes unchecked.

The most curious example poorly defined legislation is in relation to police powers to detain someone 'for the protection of other persons' under the Mental Health Act 1983 (s. 136 (1)). If the police *arrest* an individual, then that person must comply, even if the arrest is considered unlawful, and officers may use 'reasonable force' if the individual does not 'come quietly'. But whilst the Mental Health Act gives the police apparent powers to detain, there is no stated obligation put on the individual to comply, nor mention of 'reasonable force' to enforce a detention.

If the detainee told the police that they could not detain him or her, and refused to cooperate, it is not clear what the officers could lawfully do. Of more concern, people detained under this part of the Mental Health Act have fewer rights than a criminal who is being arrested – the criminal must be told what is happening and why. Those drafting the law saw a person with learning disabilities, who might be detained, as little more than a tailor's dummy.

Legislation, legal precedents and common law develop in line with the evolving values of the society they serve. If people with learning disabilities remain hidden to that society, they will have little influence over that development. The law and judicial practice will further hide the victimization of three percent of those it is supposed to serve.

unnoticed laws

Even if helpful legislation exists, such as that dealing with abuse and neglect in the Mental Health Act 1983, the police may not pursue cases or move a victim to safety because they are not familiar with specialist law. Police seem unlikely consider it their responsibility to instigate the urgent closure of a Registered Home in which residents are suffering victimization. Yet *any* person 'with reasonable grounds for concern' might apply to a magistrate for closure. The same applies to the National Assistance Act 1948. The police would only need the support of two doctors to remove a victim from an abusive situation. If professionals have failed to assess the risk of a certain activity leading to injury, Health and Safety regulations might provide a route for redress. Yet the responsibility for starting proceedings is seen as that of the Health and Safety officials, and consequently often overlooked. There is no evidence that the police ever instigate or suggest the use measures such as these.

When laws are straightforward, staff are often ignorant of their existence. Few professionals know that they might commit an offence by intercepting a letter or by instructing a colleague not to report a crime. False imprisonment by staff is a daily event in many care settings. There is little awareness that any form of unwanted touching might be an assault, or that most service-users cannot be compelled to undergo medical treatment, which would include taking an Aspirin. Certainly staff never consider that if they make an unsubstantiated accusation such as 'John hit Rubina', they may be guilty of defamation.

concealed reports

In general, crime victims would never stop to consider that something might come between them and a report to the police. Yet for people who exist in service settings, this is the point at which the barriers become bigger and even less perceptible. There is in inherent service ethos that service users should not report directly to the police.

The reporting routes for victims in service settings are usually reporting 'chains' within which one missing link can prevent a report reaching the police. Often the missing links are the perpetrators, their colleagues or friends. Reporting chains enhance the power of the perpetrator exponentially, because they mirror (for no reason related to effective reporting) line management structures. The young residential care worker who is told by a resident of a sexual assault perpetrated by the house manager often has, in theory, to report that crime to the house manager. The manager not only controls the reporting route, but also the holidays, promotion, fringe benefits, and reference of the person reporting. Is it a wonder that so many reports are concealed?

confused police responses

Inappropriate police responses to victims are unacceptable hurdles. There are too many stories of the police not taking reports by victims with learning disabilities seriously. The situation is compounded by other forms of interaction with the police. For example, one woman maintains that she would never tell the police if she had been raped, because she was treated so badly when she once went to a police station, in a spirit of helpfulness, to identify a suspect.

Police confusion between habit and law constructs another unseen barrier. The police do not usually pursue cases if victims themselves cannot make formal complaints. They claim that courts would not tolerate the absence of a victim-witness in a defended case. But it is simply custom that makes it unusual for complaints to be made by a third party, not law. In a case of murder the victim is not the complainant, nor in cases of very serious injury. Yet the principle of a third party complainant (or no complainant) is not applied when victims cannot appear as witnesses because of intellectual disability or trauma. It may be easier to achieve justice on behalf of someone who is killed than for someone who is raped. When the paradox was put to one police officer his answer was, if crude, very perceptive:

> 'You see, it's because there's no such thing as a mentally handicapped corpse.'

Why does a victim need to die before the justice system responds appropriately?

Internal police procedures for deciding if a prosecution is to be pursued are one of the least visible barriers. In one region, forms used by police to determine if an offence of 'false imprisonment' has been committed incorrectly require that the victim has suffered an injury. The type of 'false imprisonment' usually experienced by people with learning disabilities, for example being locked in a bedroom, would not usually entail injury. A police decision to drop a case could be based on incorrect vetting procedures which are concealed from public scrutiny, and are unknown to police in other regions or the Home Office.

secret gatekeepers – the CPS

Few members of the public are aware of the gatekeeping function of the Crown Prosecution Service (CPS), or even of its existence. The CPS has the power to block any case – no victim has the right to a prosecution. Decision-making is secretive and accountability is vague.

There can be contradictions between the logic of the CPS and the logic of a court. In one case a decision not to prosecute

107

was rationalized on the basis that the perpetrator was confused about the law. Yet in court ignorance of the law is not a defence. CPS officers who are unclear about a point of law can prevent a case proceeding on the basis of their opinion alone. Yet if the case reached a court, the legal arguments required to reach a decision on the same point of law may be considered to require a House of Lords ruling or even that of the European court. Judges now take account of European law when making their decisions. The CPS response to an argument based on EC law is to ignore it.

The CPS does not have the independence of the judiciary and is susceptible to ministerial influence. Through the CPS, the Home Secretary can prevent a case going to court – something that even judges do not have the power to do. Government influence over the CPS might well relate to cost-cutting. The new *Code for Crown Prosecutors* positively discourages the prosecution of minor offences. Minor offences are a significant aspect of the victimization of people with learning disabilities because they are often cumulative over a long period, sometimes by the same perpetrator. A pattern of minor victimization often represents the testing out of a vulnerable victim, then leading to serious offences. The CPS Code takes no account of cumulative, minor victimization, and the definition of 'minor' is completely within the discretion of CPS officers.

Until recently the *Code for Crown Prosecutors* positively discriminated against victims who were not convenient witnesses. CPS officers can still block cases on the basis that a person with learning disabilities will not be an adequate witness – a decision that can be taken without meeting the person concerned.

There is a further 'Catch 22'. Much of the victimization suffered by people with learning disabilities is perpetrated by people with learning disabilities. This ranges from petty assaults to grievous bodily harm and unlawful killing. The CPS is discouraged from prosecuting in this circumstance. Whilst this is a sensible line of action from the offender's perspective, no alternative remedy is provided to uphold the victim's rights. Victims of minor offences therefore also miss the chance of compensation, which might be available through a court, because the *Criminal Injuries Compensation Board* will only consider claims for major injury of over £1000.

imperceptible secondary victimization in court

If a case reaches the courts, the victim may have to battle against secondary victimization deriving from lawyers' tactics and archaic attitudes. Tactics to disconcert vulnerable witnesses are well-disguised. Such approaches as repeating the same question many times, leaving long silences, temper tantrums, congratulating witnesses on being clever, or asking a string of irrelevant questions to which the answer is 'yes' and a crucial one to which the answer is 'no', are rarely challenged. Sometimes lawyers follow a period of kind, gentle questioning by a sudden switch to aggressive confrontation. This is a known technique used by terrorist interrogators to wear down hostages. Should approaches of this nature have any place in a courtroom?

The attitudes of judges might well be even more insidious. In one case a judge likened an assault, by a professional, on a 45-year-old man to smacking a naughty child. Another judge excused an ex-policeman, who sexually assaulted his 12-year-old step daughter, on the grounds that the pregnancy of the man's wife caused 'considerable problems for a healthy young husband'. Were the problems caused to a 12-year-old girl with learning disabilities not important?

The negative effects of court cases do not stop at the end of a trial. One of the most common reasons why victims and their supporters fear going to court is because, if a case fails, the victim often then has to live (sometimes literally) with the possibility of retribution from the perpetrator. Even if a case is successful, much the same problem arises when sentences are short or non-custodial, as the perpetrator soon has open access again to the victim. This unseen barrier to justice is built on a realistic perception of secondary victimization that extends well beyond a court appearance.

hidden in crime statistics

Does the victimization of people with learning disabilities feature accurately in the profile of 'recorded crime' (police statistics)? Unlikely, because victims with learning disabilities commonly complain that police take no notice of their reports. Even if victimization is noted, it may be noted as an 'incident' rather than a crime. Such was the case when a man was pushed into a freezing river – an 'incident' that, had the man not been rescued, may well have amounted to manslaughter. If senior officers feel that a prosecution is likely to be difficult because a witness has learning disabilities, it is easy to see the temptation to avoid increasing the figures for crimes that are not 'cleared up.'

Are the statistics for 'reported crime' any better? Probably not, because interviewers for the *British Crime Survey* exclude people in group homes which are classed as 'institutions'. Even if victims live with families, it seems probable that their experiences will not constitute part of the household's response, because interviewers are not trained (or paid for the time) to ask questions in an understandable way or recognise indirect reports of uncommon offences. It seems unlikely that, 'He told me to stay in my room', or 'These girls kissed me' would be recognised as possible 'false imprisonment' and sexual assault.

Statistics for recorded crime are further skewed because much victimization suffered by service users is dealt with through forms of alternative dispute resolution. Crime relating to staff dismissals, closure of Registered Homes, formal complaints to services, and Health and Safety prosecutions does not feature in formal crime statistics. Many victim studies are based solely on police and court records, which would only reveal a fraction of the victimization that attracts formal redress.

Most statistical victim studies consider single events within a restricted time frame. One of the unique features of the victims with learning disabilities is that they have often been life-long victims. For some, victimization caused their intellectual injury in the first place, yet these people are rarely perceived as victims of crime. Often there has been no respite from abuse, starting at oppressive special schools, intensifying during years spent in hospitals, and then continuing in the form of community intimidation or victimization within community care settings. Life-history methodology would be necessary to evidence this convincingly, and victim studies are rarely, if ever, carried out in this manner.

National crime statistics influence government policy. Three per cent of the population, which suffers a very specific form of crime, is ignored in analysis that (in theory) underpins national spending priorities for crime prevention and management of the justice system. This is never recognized, when we question why the justice system is so inappropriate for individual victims with learning disabilities.

unapparent circles of negative perception

The totality of these invisible barriers greatly exceeds the sum of the constituent parts. Mutual influences culminate in a self-perpetuating circle of negative perception, which constitutes the least tangible of all the barriers.

Following the circle in one direction – negative perceptions can start with poor court practice relating to vulnerable witnesses, culminating in few convictions. This influences CPS officers, who block cases that do not fit their picture of court successes. 'A realistic prospect of conviction' is a key principle in the *Code for Crown Prosecutors* but there is, of course, little questioning as to *why* the 'prospect' might be 'unrealistic'. Police then either do not pursue cases, or recommend to the CPS that cases should not be pursued, because of their experience of how the CPS and courts have responded in the past. Victims then do not report to the police because they believe, from their previous experience or that of others, that nothing will happen. Their perception of crime and reporting becomes further confused.

Following the circle in the other direction – if victims do not recognize crime as crime, or previous experience suggests that those brokering the law may not do so, they do not report.

110

Therefore service reporting routes have never been pressured to adapt to the needs of vulnerable victims. Police practice, which is largely demand-driven, does not develop appropriately. The CPS is consequently unpractised at supporting witnesses with communication disabilities. The courts therefore end up with little experience of vulnerable witnesses. The already flawed statistical representations of the situation are further clouded, which in turn further misinforms practice and policy within the justice system.

From both directions influences meet and continue to perpetuate the circles of negative perception.

invisible in discourse

Finally, the discourse surrounding victims with learning disabilities clouds our understanding at all levels. Most significant is daily language, which is constructed by professionals and perpetuated through their power. Language that disguises what happens and obscures our view of crime, perpetrators and victims.

Women with learning disabilities are 'sexually abused' – other women are raped. Men with learning disabilities are 'physically abused' - other men are assaulted. Steal something from someone with learning disabilities and it is 'financial abuse', not theft. Police wrongfully arrest innocent members of the public, but if they do the same to someone with learning disabilities it is called 'legal abuse'. Offenders against the general community are criminals — those who victimize people with learning disabilities are 'abusers'. Victims with learning disabilities are 'survivors' and 'sufferers'. And 'sufferers' do not report crimes to the police – they 'disclose abuse' to professionals.

The press plays its part in obscuring crime against people with learning disabilities. In 1991 the *Independent* was the only national paper initially to publicize the abduction a woman with Down's Syndrome, Jo Ramsden, following the story until the discovery of her body and a subsequent trial. All other papers had ignored Ms Ramsden's disappearance, while giving a parallel story about an attractive Oxford graduate front-page coverage.

The printed word also serves to evidence the invisibility argument. Take the titles of the core literature, just from the sources to this book. From Australia, **Silent Victims**; from the US, **Violence and abuse in the lives of people with disabilities – the end of silent acceptance**. A UK local authority booklet about the abuse of vulnerable adults is entitled **Hidden victims**. The sub-editing of articles about this research provides, **Spiral of abuse and silence** and (regarding crime statistics) **Counted out of crime**. The principle training material about sexual abuse of people with learning disabilities is entitled, **Working with the unthinkable** and **It could never happen here**. The idea of invisible barriers is reflected in, **Justice means too many hurdles.** Victimization appears under press headlines such as **Secret report alleges systematic abuse of handicapped adults** (the *Independent*); **Managers tried to hide abuse** (*Observer*).

How does the invisibility argument relate to other marginalized groups? There are many parallels to the concept, discussed under the headings 'alienated', 'estranged', 'marginalized' and 'powerless' (see Williams 1993c: 838). Isolation is recognized in phrases such as 'extra-social status', 'voicelessness' and Paulo Freire's 'culture of silence'. 'Muted groups' has been used concerning women and street children, and Michele Wallace's book **Invisibility Blues** discusses black feminism (1990).

During this century victimology has progressed in its recognition of marginalized groups. Debate now specifically encompasses women, children, domestic victims, and black and minority ethic groups. The principle is the same for all – the 'invisibility' of the victims has been created by the unseen barriers between them and the achievement of justice.

VISIBLE victims

To reduce the victimization of people with learning disabilities we must see crimes as crimes, perpetrators as perpetrators and victims as victims. And then notice and question the invisible barriers in policy, practice and our minds which prevent them achieving redress.

Within the space of a few years we have torn down the Berlin wall, Northern Ireland's 'peace lines', and the barriers of apartheid, greatly enhancing global security. Surely it is not so difficult to see and dismantle the barriers that stand between people with learning disabilities and the achievement of justice, enhancing the personal security, and then in turn the visibility, of people who have been out of sight for too long. The present situation is best put by victim who has survived crime,

> 'People with learning disabilities are treated with no respect... No one believes us. It is time that criminals are taught a lesson.'

be visible

ask to be noticed.. come to light.. become visible..be seen..speak for [one's] self..attract attention.. come forward..have no secrets..live in the public eye.. stay in sight..

Roget's Thesaurus 1987

8
CHAPTER

Summary of policy considerations

CIC	Criminal Injuries Compensation
CO	Campaigning Organizations
CP	Court Practice
CPr	Crime Prevention
CPS	Crown Prosecution Service
LA	Legal Aid
LC	Law Clarification
LSPP	Local Service Policy and Practice
LR	Law Reform
NSPP	National Service-Provider Policy
PP	Police Policy

1. LAW REFORM AND CLARIFICATION

There are few arguments to support the need for special legislation relating to victims with intellectual disability, except an insistence that the anti-discrimination elements of European law (see Chap.6) should apply to the legislative framework of the UK. However, some aspects of existing legislation are now inappropriate or unclear, because they were drafted before community care was widespread and did not envisage the 'ordinary lifestyles' of people with intellectual disabilities.

The policy proposals specifically relate to

1.1 Concerning **abduction**, the Sexual Offences Act 1956 has three shortcomings:

    1.   it does not include the abduction of men

    2.   it assumes that all people with learning disabilities are in 'the possession' of a guardian, and so, for example, may exclude abduction from a flat or other form of independent living

    3.   it omits the possibility of abduction for sexual offences between women. [Chap.1, p.4]

LR

113

The policy proposals specifically relate to

1.2 Legislation concerning **sexual relations** and people with learning disabilities needs reviewing. In its present form it:

LR

- relies greatly on the term 'mental defect' which, although defined in the Mental Health Act 1983, is often inappropriate and offensive

- can make healthy, consenting relationships unlawful, particularly homosexual. Present legislation creates disabilities for carers and staff who may wish to assist people with learning disabilities to have consenting sexual relationships

- could deter the reporting of sexual offences because of the implied responsibility put on managers and staff to monitor and control sexual behaviour

- is gender-biased in a way that does not reflect what is now known about sexual offences against men. For example the Mental Health Act 1983 makes it an offence 'for a man to have unlawful sexual intercourse with a woman who is a mentally disordered patient', but does not mention sexual offences by men against men, or by women against men or women. The Mental Health Act 1959 (s128(a)) should be amended to include sexual assault (as well as sexual intercourse) and offences by female staff

- does not embrace offences committed in other countries except, curiously, concerning the prostitution of women. [Chap.1, p.7]

1.3 The law concerning **indecent exposure** has a weakness that is specific to the lives of people in care settings – it only relates to exposure in a public place or if the act can be seen from a public place. Indecent exposure by, for example, a member of staff in a group home, might not be included. [Chap.1, pp.6–7]

LC

1.4 The extent to which the Public Order Act applies to the quasi-public areas of group homes needs to be clarified, because the Act was conceived before deinstitutionalization and Community Care legislation created new, indeterminate forms of 'dwelling'. [Chap.1 p.8]

LC

Similarly, are group homes 'public places' within the terms of the Mental Health Act 1983 (s136(1))? If not the practice of police removing people 'for the protection of other persons' is unlawful. It is also unclear as to whether the person being detained must comply, and it is questionable that such a person has fewer rights than someone being arrested (for example, to be told what is happening). [Chap.2, p.31; Chap.7]

114

The policy proposals specifically relate to

1.5 The degree to which the Mental Health Act 1983 (s.127), concerning ill-treatment or wilful neglect, relates to settings that are not designated a Health Service 'hospital or home', yet the individuals concerned are under Health Service care, needs to be clarified. [Chap.1, p.11]   **LC**

1.6 The administration of the Vaccine Damage Payments Act 1979 should be reviewed urgently.   [Chap.1, p.16]   **LR**

1.7 The Congenital Disabilities Act 1976 could usefully be revised in the light of American experience, increased scientific knowledge about *in utero* damage, and the growth of the drug culture since the time the legislation came into being. [Chap.1, p.16]   **LR**

1.8 State mobility benefits should be reviewed to include the 'protective use' of taxis and special transport schemes by people who may be vulnerable because of intellectual disabilities. [Chap.3, p.45]   **LC**

1.9 People with learning disabilities are frequently the victims of minor assaults by other people with learning disabilities, and these cases do not usually reach the courts. This precludes the possibility of compensation through the courts, and, unless the injury is severe enough to attract compensation in excess of £1000, the CICB will not make a payment. This 'Catch 22' could be remedied by making CICB compensation available for minor injuries if the case has not been taken to court because the offender is 'mentally disordered'. (This would, of course, apply to any victim.) [Chap 6, p.95]   **LC**   **CIC**

1.10 Legal Aid should be made available to individuals who require representation at an inquest, if a case is a public interest concern because of the implication of public services. [Chap. 6, p.97]   **LC**   **LA**

2. PREVENTION

People with learning disabilities are far from being helpless victims. General preventive strategies should be based on their very considerable knowledge and abilities. However, for the present, preventive strategies will inevitably be bound up with service policy, and much low-level victimization could be prevented by a more active 'safety first' ethos in service settings.

The policy proposals specifically relate to

2.1   Basic crime prevention strategies should include: **CPr**   **LSPP**

- education based on existing awareness and life-experiences
- the protective use of transport
- learning avoidance strategies
- encouraging a visible police presence amongst people with learning disabilities
- an awareness of avoiding 'advertising' vulnerability
- a recognition that people with learning disabilities can be part of general crime prevention in the community. [Chap.3, p.43]

2.2   Recognizing and dealing with abduction attempts should   **CPr**   **LSPP**
       be a key element in personal safety training, for women
       and men. [Chap.1. p.3]

2.3   If people with learning disabilities are helped to recognize   **CPr**
       when they might be 'tested out' by abusers, and taught
       how to respond,   more serious incidents may be
       avoided. [Chap.3, p.53]

2.4   When people move into community settings, part of their   **LSPP**
       education programme should include an awareness of
       what crime is and of the possibilities of getting a criminal
       record for behaviour that may have been 'accepted' as
       normal in hospital. [Chap.3, p.47]

2.5   Managers should introduce a 'safety first' policy in all   **LSPP**
       service settings. If this means one-to-one staffing to
       prevent victimization between people with learning
       disabilities, this is probably more cost-effective in the
       long-run than resorting to secure units and dealing with
       the trauma or resultant challenging behaviour of victims.
       [Chap. 3, p.47]

2.6   The relationship between victimization and resultant   **LSPP**
       behaviour disabilities should underlie personal safety
       policies within service settings. [Chap.3, p.52]

2.7   If there is a single strategy that would reduce the amount   **LSPP**
       low-level victimization in the lives of people with learning
       disabilities, it is proper staff training about what
       constitutes an unlawful act. [Chap.2, p.19]

- Appropriate induction can increase staff and volunteer awareness of offences they might unknowingly commit, and of actions by others that should be treated as offences. [Chap.3, p.48]

The policy proposals specifically relate to

- Staff can be advised that if they feel they cannot do their job without the possibility of committing offences, or other people committing offences, this should be communicated directly to senior management in writing. [Chap.3, p.48]

- Trade unions might usefully inform their members about the law in relation to their job. They should also negotiate with managers to ensure that employees are not forced into circumstances where they, or anyone else, might commit offences. [Chap.3, p.48]

2.8 If police checks on potential staff are considered desirable, service providers may consider introducing a policy that all staff are employed generically, i.e. on the basis that any employee might be called upon to work with children and therefore will be checked. [Chap.3, p.49]

LSPP   **NSPP**

2.9 'Minor' victimization can reinforce perpetrators' impressions of their power and a victim's comparative weakness, potentially leading to more serious crimes. This highlights the importance of identifying and remedying minor injustice, especially by staff. [Chap.3, p.53]

CPr

3. REPORTING

Effective reporting is the key to achieving justice for victims. It is crucial that incidents that are currently conceptualized by staff and carers as merely 'abuse' (a medical or social problem), should be seen and responded to as crimes, if that is what they are.

The principle that victims should have an unfettered right to report, or have a report made, directly to the police is not well-established. There needs to be change of attitude within service settings and the police to encourage and respond positively to reporting. The crucial question should not be whether or not to report to the police but how the police and CPS then respond. (Chap.4, p.55)

3.1 Failing to report a crime because of a belief, or threat, that police involvement will worsen a situation is very questionable. Such a decision may appear negligent in the light of future, perhaps more serious, circumstances. [Chap.4, p.56]

LSPP

3.2 Proper liaison with police about how incidents should be reported, before emergencies arise, is essential. [Chap.4, p.57]

LSPP

The policy proposals specifically relate to

3.3 Despite the few people who make false allegations, the only safe policy is that all allegations are investigated. Investigations and suspensions should be a normal and accepted part of being a professional, but there should be a quick and efficient channel for investigations. [Chap.4, p.57]

LSPP

3.4 The trend towards mandatory reporting to the police, by staff, and of ensuring the protection of staff who report, should become standard practice. [Chap.4, p.59]

LSPP   **NSPP**

3.5 In accord with the British Psychological Society guidelines, any mention of criminal offences should be reported to an appropriate third party, regardless of issues of confidentiality, unless there is absolute certainty that no person's safety or interests will ever be threatened as a result of not reporting. [Chap.4, p.60]

LSPP

3.6 It is useful to decide, with police, an outline policy when victims do not want a prosecution against offenders. [Chap.4, p.61]

LSPP

3.7 Service users should be generally aware that staff have a duty to care and therefore must report anything that might threaten the safety or interests of others or themselves. [Chap.4, p.64]

LSPP

3.8 Managers should ensure that service users have access to reporting 'webs' rather than reporting 'chains' in which one 'missing link' can prevent the possibility of achieving justice. [Chap.4, p.65]

LSPP

3.9 The tradition of staff and service users not reporting directly to the police should be questioned. [Chap.4, p.69]

LSPP

3.10 Staff need to know exactly whom to contact in a police station - a named officer, the child protection team or domestic violence unit. Reports need to be free of jargon, and stress urgency if appropriate. [Chap.4, p.70]

LSPP

4.   THE POLICE

Community care has introduced a significant new 'victim-group' to the police. Understandably, whilst there are islands of excellence, general police practice still requires development. This is particularly important in circumstances that may be seen by individual officers as reasonable practice, but may be experienced by people with learning disabilities as direct victimization. [Chap.2 p.31]

The policy proposals specifically relate to

4.1   Although Public Order Offences are the most common form of victimization reported by people with learning disabilities, not one instance of a prosecution is known. A greater awareness of the Act is necessary amongst professionals and family carers, and there should be an insistence that police make use of Public Order legislation. [Chap.1, p.9] — **LSPP**   **PP**

4.2   Victimization and inappropriate actions from the police usually stem from two problems — **PP**

- failure to recognise that a victim or suspect has learning disabilities

- an absence of knowledge about sources of support and expertise within the country. [Chap.2, p.34]

4.3   All officers investigating complaints by vulnerable victims should follow the basic precept that initially any story, however improbable, should be accepted at face value, without any intimation of disbelief or that the matter is too minor for police involvement. If a complaint turns out to be improper this should be explained with great care, after a full investigation. [Chap.2, p.34] — **PP**

4.4   A decision not to pursue an inquiry or prosecution, on the grounds that a victim has learning disabilities should, as a matter of policy, not be taken by individual, 'front-line' police officers. [Chap.2, p.34] — **PP**

4.5   Regional procedures, providing guidance to police officers about the decision to prosecute, should be monitored nationally to ensure that — **PP**

1.   the law is correctly and unambiguously interpreted
2.   the advice does not work against the equitable achievement of justice for vulnerable people because of the special nature of some of the offences that they commonly suffer, for example the 'false imprisonment' of people in care settings. [Chap.4, p.69]

4.6   The role of an appropriate adult for victims and witnesses should be reviewed to ensure consistency throughout the UK, from initial interviews through to court hearings. [Chap.4, p.71] — **LC**   **PP**

4.7   Police should not fail to pursue a case because a victim cannot make a formal complaint. [Chap.4, p.71] — **LC**   **PP**

119

The policy proposals specifically relate to

5. THE JUSTICE SYSTEM

It is arguable that the justice system has the most to learn about meeting the needs of victims with learning disabilities – at present few cases reach the courts and there is little practical experience amongst the officials concerned. In general, reform does not require radical legislative change but a more benign use of existing frameworks.

5.1 Courts might note that delays inevitably favour the defendant, especially if witnesses have learning disabilities. [Chap.5, p.77]

    CP

5.2 The degree to which existing precedents concerning the use of video for adults in court relate to vulnerable victim-witnesses should be made explicit. But, in the long-term, reducing the level of intimidation experienced in court seems preferable to widespread use of video links. [Chap.5, p.87]

    LC   **CP**

5.3 There should be an assumption that witnesses with learning disabilities are competent, both in law and in practice, and the burden of proof for determining otherwise should be put on the party challenging competence. [Chap.5, p.81]

    LR

5.4 Assessments of IQ should not, alone, be used to determine an individual's competence, as it is established that this is inappropriate concerning *suspects* with learning disabilities. [Chap.5, p.81, p.88]

    LC   **CP**

5.5 The oath is an archaic, illogical and sometimes farcical aspect of court practice which demonstrably works against the achievement of justice for people with learning disabilities. Recent appeal rulings suggest the possibility that a person with learning disabilities could read a personal oath or affirmation, written in a language that is understood, and that this would be lawful. This point should be clarified, and appended to the Judicial Studies Board guidelines – *Oaths and Oath-Taking* (JSB 1994). [Chap.5, p.81]

    LR   **LC**

5.6 Careful summing-up of evidence, by judges, is preferable to proposals for psychological assessments of the reliability of an individual's evidence, not least because the decision about whom to assess is arbitrary and can itself cast doubt about the reliability of an individual in the mind of a jury. [Chap.5, p.84]

    CP

120

The policy proposals specifically relate to

5.7 The international move away from arbitrary assessments of admissibility and reliability towards a mandatory requirement to assist communication should be followed. [Chap.5, p.84]

LR   **CP**

5.8 Legal Aid should automatically be available to help people with any form of communication problems – at present it seems to be available at the court's discretion for those with obvious impairments or when there are language disabilities. Aid should ensure that the support permitted from a lay advocate or 'appropriate adult' to assist with communication should be consistent from the point of initial police investigation to appearance in court, for offenders or victims. [Chap.5, p.84]

LC   **CP**

5.9 The UK *Code for Crown Prosecutors* clearly discourages redress for victims if, in the opinion of the CPS, an offence is minor. This does not acknowledge the nature of victimization against people with learning disabilities, which is often an on-going and cumulative history of 'minor' offences, sometimes by the same perpetrator. The CPS should take into consideration the opinion of the victim as to what is minor. [Chap.5, p.53, Chap.6, p.86]

CPS

5.10 The *Nova Scotia Protocol for Investigation and prosecution of cases involving persons with special communication needs* (1991) provides an exemplary framework which could readily be applied in the UK. Its principal merits are that it:

CPS   **CP**

- puts the emphasis on assisting communication

- views police procedure, prosecution service practice, and court procedure as a whole

- gives the prosecution service the responsibility for preparing vulnerable witnesses

- is written in a style that positively encourages the achievement of justice for vulnerable victims, which is in contrast to the UK *Code for Crown Prosecutors*. [Chap.6, p.85]

5.11 There are suggestions that victims with learning disabilities should be accorded separate legal status in the courts. It seems unlikely that this could be done simply and conclusively, and would, in any case, be contrary to the philosophy of 'ordinary living' and the wishes of many victim-witnesses. [Chap.6, p.87]

LR

The policy proposals specifically relate to

5.12   Specific responsibility should be given to the clerk in magistrates' courts, to identify petty offenders with learning disabilities, to ensure that magistrates seek a proper assessment, and to propose appropriate diversionary measures.   [Chap.2, p.35]

CP

6.   GENERAL

6.1   The insurance policies of service providers, in relation to residential settings, should include the property of residents, if that is what the residents wish. [Chap.1, p.13]

LSPP

6.2   If an offender with learning disabilities is likely to receive a custodial sentence, the probation service and defence solicitor should be reminded of the possibility of using a Guardianship Order (Mental Health Act 1983, s.37). [Chap.2, p25]

LSPP   **CP**

6.3   Statutory bodies, voluntary organizations, and campaigning organizations should consider private prosecution if the police or CPS seem to be blocking a case unreasonably, because this could set precedents for criminal proceedings in the future and directly challenge questionable police and CPS practice. [Chap.5, p.75]

CO

6.4   An awareness of European human rights law should influence all decisions concerning the achievement of justice for people with learning disabilities.   The possibility of appeals to the European court should, if appropriate, be indicated in all discussions. [Chap.6, p.98]

LSPP   **CO**

6.5   The practice of deducting CICB or court compensation from state benefits should be reviewed.   [Chap.6, p.95]

LR   **CIC**

6.6   National crime surveys and police crime statistics should not exclude victims with learning disabilities.   [Chap.7]

CO   **PP**

1
APPENDIX

Outline material for police training

Time constraints on police training are unlikely to permit a significant input about victims with learning disabilities. However, it is possible to integrate the main messages into existing training syllabuses. Therefore, rather than rigid proposals for police training, Appendix I outlines the main learning points, concerning **attitudes** towards people with learning disabilities, illustrated with case stories.

Awareness of the nature of victimization against people with learning disabilities, and how the law should relate, can be gained from Chapter 1, and an awareness of the likely perpetrator groups from Chapter 2.

Discussion of **technical** points can be found in Chapter 2 p.31, Chapter 4, p.69, and the policy recommendations concerning the police p.118. The recognition sheet on p.33 is particularly relevant.

A video and transcript, which includes victims with learning disabilities describing what happened to them, is available as part of the *Cracking Crime* training pack (Pavilion Publishing, Brighton, 1995). This may help officers to learn that a report which may at first sound muddled and incomprehensible may well constitute a reliable statement − if the officer listens carefully. The video also teaches that people with learning disabilities are far from being helpless victims − they have abilities which permit them to be an active part of the public response to crime.

Responding to reports

There is concern that 'front line' officers do not respond to the victimization of people with learning disabilities in the way they would for other members of the community. Whether this be true or not, there are instances where most officers would agree that responses could have been better.

Case 1
A man with learning disabilities in a rural area was, on one occasion, the victim of a hit-and-run driver, and on another, gored by a bull. In both cases the officer concerned did not visit the man because of what was judged to be his inability to give a statement. As it happens the man's sister is a police officer in another force – complaints were swift.

- **Officers should not prejudge an individual's ability to make a statement (nor to put right the injustice of being ignored!)**

- **There is a growing feeling that the justice system has a direct responsibility to overcome communication problems for people with learning disabilities, as it must for those who do not speak English well.**

- **Child Protection Teams, or other specialists, can often help.**

- **Over 3% of officers with families will have children with learning disabilities. These officers can often be a useful resource.**

Case 2
A group home frequently suffered from minor crime – stones thrown through windows, litter and excrement put in the garden, and arson attempts. Staff complained to one officer about the poor response from the local station. He later advised them that when they phoned the police they should just give the address of the house, and no indication that it was a group home, because this led to reports being ignored.

- **Even if an immediate response is not possible, complaints should not be ignored because of a feeling that the victims are not full members of the community.**

- **Although technically this type of offence is probably against the Social or Health Services department, the victims are the residents of the house. Victim support involvement would often be appropriate.**

Case 3
A phone call was received, by a local station, from a social worker stating, *'A woman with learning disabilities has just disclosed to me that she was abused.'* Police took four days to respond to what turned out to be a report of rape.

- **Social workers and other professionals sometimes use jargon that can obscure the urgency or importance of a case.**

Case 4
A woman with learning disabilities relates how a drunken man knocked at her front door when she was alone, one evening and frightened her. In a another incident, youths were running around the garden shouting abuse. The police were called on both occasions but there was no response. Offences under the Public Order Act were probably committed, and there was the likelihood of repeated victimization. The woman is now very scared to be at home on her own, causing considerable problems for her elderly parents.

- **If someone with learning disabilities calls the police, to them, the incident is serious. Rarely will the police be contacted just to complain.**

- **Even if an immediate response is not possible some recognition of the incident, and reassurance that the woman was right to call the police, is necessary.**

Cases 5 and 6

A woman with learning disabilities noticed that her dog was very excited about something in the garden. She investigated and saw three men breaking into the house next door. She called the police, who attended quickly and caught the intruders. When asked how she elicited such a quick response she replied, *'I just told them to shift their arses and get round here – so they came.'*

A man with learning disabilities, who worked at a DIY store, thought one of the customers looked suspicious, and pointed him out to the manager. Sure enough he stole something, and was apprehended. When asked why he became concerned he replied, *'He was wearing sun-glasses inside the shop. I've seen about people like him on Crimewatch.'*

· **Many people with learning disabilities have a high awareness of crime, and are well able to assist prevention.**

Attending Incidents

There is often an element of surprise when front-line officers encounter a victim with learning disabilities. Wrong judgements can seriously affect the efficacy of police work, and hinder the efforts of specialist units.

Case 1

In a Hertfordshire village, police attended an incident between two men, in an alleyway between shops. They found a large man with learning disabilities sitting on a youth, pinning him to the ground. Both were blood stained. It turned out that the man with learning disabilities had been attacked by three youths, who broke his glasses and caused him facial and other injuries. He sat on one of them to prevent escape, waiting for the police to come. He required hospital attention and several stitches to his face. A guilty plea was obtained, because of the strength of forensic evidence and witness statements.

· **The officers attending this incident could easily have assumed that the man with learning disabilities was the offender. They might have arrested him or lost the opportunity to obtain good evidence.**

· **Careful use of evidence prevented the trauma of a court appearance for the man with learning disabilities.**

Case 2

A man with learning disabilities suffered a burglary at his flat on a Saturday evening. Police attended quickly, although there was little hope of catching anyone. Before they left they contacted the council, to get the broken lock repaired, and called the duty social worker. They carefully checked what was stolen, including food and cash, and ensured that the man was not in disabilities over the weekend because of his losses.

· **Crime prevention following an incident may need to be more than simple advice; likewise, the need for immediate victim support.**

Case 3

A woman who was mugged and had her handbag stolen did not report this to staff at her house. Three days later it was noticed that she had a broken arm. Officers had caught suspects with the handbag, but they could not proceed because the woman, although able to communicate quite well, would not state clearly that they had stolen it from her (the suspects claimed they had just found it).

· **Questioning needs to be very structured, remembering that some people with learning disabilities may not have a clear concept of crime.**

· **Crime prevention work with people with learning disabilities needs to emphasize, in a very obvious manner (i.e. with appropriate examples) what a crime is.**

Case 4

In a case of alleged rape, a woman withdrew her accusation after pressure from her family. The suspect turned out to be the boyfriend of the woman's cousin.

· **There are many reasons why family members may wish to cover up an incident. Even simple embarrassment related to the victim's disability can underlie a request to take no action.**

Case 5
A man who went to the Post Office to collect his pension was persuaded by a young woman to hand over his money on the promise of her buying a bike for him. The officers who attended said they could achieve very little but commented that *'People like him should not be allowed out on his own.'*

· **Whilst crime prevention advice is a valuable aspect of police responses, comments suggesting that the way for someone to avoid crime is to stay at home are very questionable. This form of advice would, for example, be completely unacceptable if made about young women or someone from a minority ethnic group. It is equally misguided when made about people with learning disabilities.**

General interaction between police and people with learning disabilities

Much interaction between officers and people with learning disabilities will not be formal, but can have a great influence on how an individual views the police and crime generally.

Cases 1 and 2
At a discussion about rape, a young woman with learning disabilities said categorically that she would never go to the police if she was raped. When asked why, she said that a few weeks earlier she had been asked to try and identify someone from police files at the local station and they had been very rude to her (perhaps frustration at her slowness).

A young man stated that he would never, ever ask the police for help. He told how he once been walking across a pedestrian crossing when a car approached fast and the driver shouted, *'Get off the road you idiot.'* It was a police car.

· **Every interaction with the police is important**

Case 3
Allegedly, a care assistant had extracted large sums from the building society account of a man with learning disabilities. Police were involved but the matter was difficult to prove. However the man's mother was very positive about the police work: *'I think the police had an entirely beneficial effect on John. Nice as they were, they made him realize it was a serious matter and he had to take some responsibility for looking after his own affairs.'*

· **Conviction should not be seen as the only successful outcome of a case. Sensitive police work can have many other beneficial effects.**

Case 4
Police attended an incident where a man with learning disabilities, who lives alone in a flat, claimed that he had been assaulted by a neighbour. The facts were hard to obtain and the officers concluded, probably quite reasonably, that both parties were in part to blame. They told the two men to *'Stop acting like children'*. Because of this comment the man concerned has lost all respect for the police and, although frequently victimized, is very unwilling for police involvement.

· **People with learning disabilities are sometimes very sensitive about being likened to children - it happens all to frequently as a form of abuse. Although the officers' handling of this incident was probably very well judged, the comment had long-term consequences.**

Crime between people with learning difficulties

When both victim and victimizer have learning disabilities, there is a dilemma. There is need to uphold the rights of the victim, as for any citizen. But over-reaction can lead to victimization of the offender which far exceeds any wrong done, or to responses from the justice system which are ineffective and probably inspire further problem behaviour. Increasingly the CPS are not proceding with cases against people with learning disabilities. There is a growing feeling that people with learning disabilities living in the community should not be protected from the consequences of their actions, but it is a general principal that punishment is not appropriate if its meaning is not understood by the offender.

Case 1

A woman from a day centre visited the home of another woman from the same centre, and stole five pounds. A complaint was made to the police, and officers responded by first discussing the matter with the manager of the centre. It was agreed that the suspect should be interviewed by uniformed officers. She admitted taking the money, and was informally cautioned, with an agreement to pay back the sum by weekly instalments.

- **The officers arrived at an effective solution which upheld the rights of the victim, made the point to the offender that an offence had been committed, but did not exacerbate the matter. Senior officers should give credit for good police work of this nature, even if it does not result in higher conviction statistics.**

Case 2

In a case of a minor assault, between two men with learning disabilities, the police took the offender to the station, showed him the cells, took him to the court room and told him to stand in the dock. They pointed out that this is what would happen to him, if charges were pressed by the victim.

- **If it results from consultation with professionals, this type of action can be effective. But if applied without thought, it could cause trauma far in excess of the original offence, or create further behaviour problems in the offender.**

Case 3

A man living in a group home ended up in hospital after another resident poured boiling water over him. Officers from a domestic violence unit attended, but no further action was taken. The man concludes, *'Now if I had done something like that to someone outside, I would have been locked up.'*

- **Even if further action is not appropriate, it should be made clear to victims that they have been the victim of a crime. Victim Support should be contacted, and Criminal Injuries Compensation considered.**

Crime by staff

Victimisation by staff with a duty to care is common, especially sexual offences.

Case 1

Staff and residents at one group home stripped a new resident, tied him to a table, beat and sexually assaulted him, because he had a record of sexual offences. No report was made to the police.

Case 2

Staff at a London hostel *'were alleged to have kissed, shouted at, and locked up residents. One member of staff had to be prevented from putting a resident in a bath mixed with bleach and disinfectant'.*

It was two years later before other staff reported this, and even then not to the police. Eventually the matter was taken up by an MP.

Case 3

Abuse at one group home included residents being beaten, pulled along the floor by their hair, and locked in their rooms. Police became aware of these incidents because a student social worker had expressed concern to her tutor and the local paper had reported the story.

- **There are many reasons why staff do not report directly to the police – fear of recrimination or loss of promotion, an assumption that someone else will take action, lack of recognition that certain actions may constitute crimes, misguided ideas of confidentiality.**

- **Indications of victimization will often come from indirect sources.**

Case 4

A care assistant, who received a five-year prison sentence for sexually assaulting two women, was caught because a chance remark was followed up by a social worker. The offender told the women that if they told anyone what was happening they would not be believed and they would end up being *'sent to a mental hospital'.*

- **Staff have immense power over those they care for. Older people who have lived in long-stay hospitals will often recall punitive regimes and lives made miserable by staff. It may be necessary to ascertain and dispel fears before interviewing victims, and to interview without professionals present in a place that is not related to service settings.**

Offender-victims

Although the above examples do not relate to offenders with learning disabilities, it is worth noting that offenders also are, or can become, victims in many circumstances.

Cases 1 and 2
A young man with learning disabilities, who was convicted of exposing himself to a young child, was eventually given a Guardianship Order (i.e. to live under close Social Services supervision in a hostel). In the interim he was held in prison, where he was sexually assaulted, and beaten up.

A male resident at a hostel allegedly sexually assaulted a female resident. He was arrested, charged and spent several weeks in prison. Charges were dropped because of insufficient forensic evidence and the assumption that the victim would not be an adequate witness. Even if convicted, a prison sentence would have been very unlikely.

- **An offender with learning disabilities is unlikely to receive a prison sentence, but is likely to suffer if held on remand in a prison. The defence solicitor and CPS should be encouraged to make appropriate bail arrangements including Mental Health Act 1983 (s37) (see page 25).**

- **Action which means that a suspect with learning disabilities is held in prison should be avoided if there is no possibility of a case proceeding.**

Case 3
A pleasant young man in a residential home stated, *'I did a crime - criminal damage. I kicked in two windows. I got taken to the station and locked up for ten hours. Then I got a caution.'* When asked why he did this he said, *'This kid I knew threw a cup of coffee over me and I got upset. But you can't take it out on a twelve-year-old can you? So I took it out on them windows.'*

- **Offending is sometimes reasonable, rational behaviour when viewed in a broader perspective.**

Case 4
A young man who was seen by staff as *'difficult'* and *'irresponsible'* had been charged with a minor public order offence. At a case meeting the psychologist suggested that he could *'Go and live in a cardboard box on the streets... If he could find one.'* Also that he should cut his leg off and get a wooden one so that he had something to blame for all his failings.

From a private discussion with the young man later, he said that he had once been beaten up and locked in a fridge when working with McDonald's. When asked if anything else bad had ever happened to him he said: *'Oh yes – when I was 14 I was raped. I had reading and writing lessons with this woman and when she wasn't there her bloke, he was 40, raped me. My girlfriend told a community policeman we knew. My dad said we could not go to court because I wouldn't get things right in court.'*

- **It is often assumed wrongly that, because a person is in care, their background is known to professionals and recorded.**

- **It is also assumed that the professionals contribute rational advice which will help a person to understand the world better.**

2

APPENDIX

Outline of a training session for service staff and lay advocates

Many ideas for staff training are included throughout the book, and these can be easily integrated into existing training programmes.

Appendix 1 outlines a programme for a training session exclusively about the victimization of people with learning disabilities, which ideally should be co-presented by victims or potential victims.

The learning pack *Cracking Crime* (Pavilion Publishers: 8 St George's Place, Brighton, BN1 4GB) includes a video, *Crime against people with learning disabilities*, which would illustrate the main themes of the training session, and learning material for people with learning disabilities, which would form a basis for discussing prevention and coping skills.

All material in *Invisible Victims* and *Cracking Crime* may be photocopied or produced as OHPs, on a 'one-off' basis for training sessions. If material is to be reproduced in bulk (50+), or to appear in another publication, permission must be sought from the publishers.

Crime and abuse against people with learning disabilities

The training session will cover

1. the type of victimization that occurs and how the law relates to it

2. who the perpetrators are (including victimization between people with learning disabilities)

3. prevention

4. reporting

5. using the courts

6. alternatives to the criminal system

7. learning coping skills (for potential victims).

The aim of the session is to

- reduce the 'invisibility' of victimization against people with learning disabilities

- identify what is special about the victimization of people with learning disabilities

- provide a basis for those attending to develop

> personal skills
>
> local policies
>
> their own training materials.

TRAINER NOTES

NOTE
The recommended use of the video, *Crime against people with learning disabilities* follows the same sequence as the video itself. Stop the video at the correct place and restart for the next sequence. The contents page of the video workbook provides an outline, and the left hand pages of the book a transcript.

1. **What sort of victimization occurs and how the law relates to it**

Aim: to generate an awareness of 'the problem' and that many taken-for-granted events in the lives of people with learning disabilities are more than abuse – they are clearly crimes. Staff and advocates should then feel more confident about insisting on appropriate police responses.

to emphasise that staff have a duty to gain an awareness about the law concerning minor offences.

to remind that even if offences appear minor in the light of what happens generally, the fact that they are **offences** establishes boundaries necessary to uphold the rights of people with learning disabilities.

Use:
i   *Invisible Victims* – Chapter 1 and Chapter 3, p.50–51
ii   Video – *What is a crime*: discussion in the pub, headline crimes, everyday crimes.
iii 'Which of these events might be a crime' at the end of this section.

2. **Who the perpetrators are (including victimization between people with learning disabilities)**

Aim: to emphasize that perpetrators do not fit the normal preconceptions of 'criminals' and that this can cloud the ability to recognize victimization, especially if the perpetrator has learning disabilities.

Use:
i   *Invisible Victims* Chapter 2

3. **Prevention**

Aim: to create an awareness of the range of preventive strategies relating both to potential victims and the environments in which they exist.

Use:
i   *Invisible Victims* Chapter 3
ii   Materials available from the local police crime prevention units

4. Reporting

Aims: to encourage direct reporting to the police and the setting up of networks between police and services to respond to this;

to discuss the question of confidentiality and understand the British Psychological Society guidelines in relation to crime against clients.

to demonstrate that currently, reporting routes for victims in service settings are 'chains' (reflecting line-management structures) and one missing link can block a report, instead of 'webs' providing a variety of options.

to show staff how to report without jeopardizing their jobs, if necessary through the organization Public Concern at Work.

Use:
i   *Invisible Victims* Chapter 4
ii   Video – *What is a crime*: how to tell, who to tell;
        Getting Justice: contact the police, in the police station.

5. Using the courts

Aims: to create an awareness that it **is** possible to take cases through the courts for victims with learning disabilities

to develop a basic knowledge of how a court works

to highlight the need for people with learning disabilities to experience courts, (by observing from the public gallery or pre-arranged visits) **before** they are victims,

Use:
i   *Invisible Victims* Chapter 5.
ii   Video - *Getting Justice*: the Crown Prosecution Service, the court, who's in court, giving evidence, witnesses are called, the decision
iii **The Courts Charter** (Lord Chancellor's department 1992)
iv   **The Victims Charter** (Home Office 1990)

6. Alternatives to the criminal system

Aim: to increase awareness of the range of options available for achieving justice for victims and when these might be appropriate.

Use:
i   *Invisible Victims* Chapter 6

7. Learning coping skills (for potential victims)

Aims: to increase awareness of existing support networks for victims

to demonstrate the skills potential victims can learn through roleplay and discussion

Use:
i   Video - *Getting together*
ii   *Cracking crime* (learning pack). Practising some of the roleplays would make a constructive but relaxed ending to the session.

Conclusion:
Get each participant to list three ways of starting a 'Safety First' campaign for potential victims with whom they work or advocate.

Which of these events might be a crime?

1   John works part-time. Each month his pay cheque is sent, by post, to the group home where he lives. The manager always spots when the cheque arrives, and takes it from the mail box and puts it straight in John's post office account for him.

2   Karen is always shouting. At her home everyone decides that when she shouts she will be sent to her room for half an hour and told to stay there.

3   Usha is always late for meals. The manager where she lives usually tells the others to hold her hand and pull her gently towards the dining room, although often she does not seem to want to go.

4   Mohamed is a very friendly volunteer. Fatma does not talk or smile. It is Fatma's birthday and Mohamed gives her a big hug and a kiss, she tries to back off, but he does not let go.

5   On outings to the park, John is always last to get back into the mini-van. Fred, the father of another man, shouts at him, 'Come on you cretin, if you don't get in the bus quickly, I'll come over there, tie you up and carry you in.'

6   A young worker is sitting in the office at a group home. A woman who has spilt some tea will not stop laughing. He shakes his fist at her, and says 'It's not funny. You could burn yourself.'

7   Most of the men at one group home like football, so the staff put aside £1.50 each week from their benefits so that every month they can all go to a match.

8   John swears a lot in the house, so the others decide that he will be fined 20p each time he does it.

9   The staff at Mary's house are very concerned about her safety, because they live in a rough area. They tell her that if she is not back by 11.00pm, she will be locked out.

10 School children throw mud at Peter when he leaves his day centre, but he does not get hit by it.

Which of these events might be a crime? – Answers

Technically, all these scenarios might depict a criminal act.

It is very unlikely that the police would charge the perpetrator for offences of this nature. However if these and similar events happened regularly, they could form the basis for staff dismissal, a case of 'wilful neglect or ill-treatment' under the Mental Health Act 1983 (s127), closure of a registered home, or a civil action for neglect.

Reasons:

1   Intercepting a letter by post is an offence (see Chapter 2, p.21)

2   Compelling someone to stay in a room is a 'false imprisonment' (see Chapter 1, p.11)

3   Any form of unwanted touching is technically assault and battery (see Chapter 1, p.4)

4   Again, unwanted touching is an assault, and in this case arguably a sexual assault. This example would also probably be an offence against Islamic law, particularly as the man is Moslem and should know better.

5   This could be a Public Order offence because there was an insult and a clear threat of violence.

6   This could be a technical assault if it was clear that the woman feared violence - an assault does not need to entail touching (see Chapter 1, p.4).

7   Staff should not use a person's benefits for communal activities unless to do so is clearly the individual's choice or permitted by a legal guardian.

8   Any system of fines would be unlawful unless the individual had accepted this as part of a 'membership' agreement (as when joining a library). It is unlikely that any such agreement would be lawful concerning a person's home.

9   Again, this is likely to be 'false imprisonment'.

10   Under the public Order Act 1986 s8 it is an offence to throw a missile even if it falls short (Chapter 1, p.9).

References

Allington, C. L. J. (1992) 'Sexual abuse within services for people with learnng disabilities', *Mental Handicap*, 20, pp.59–63.

Ashton, G. and Ward, A. (1992) *Mental Handicap and the Law*, London: Sweet and Maxwell.

Berger, M. (1991) 'Behind bars before birth', *Observer*, 18 August, p.44.

BIMH (1992) *Sexual Abuse: Where Do We Go From Here? Bulletin No.86,* Clevedon: British Institute of Mental Handicap.

Bligh, S. and Kupperman, P. (1993) 'Brief report: facilitated communication evaluation procedure accepted in a court case', *Journal of Autism and Development Disorders*, 23, 3, pp.553–557.

British Psychological Society (1985) *Code of Conduct for Psychologists*, London: British Psychological Society.

Brown, H. and Craft, A. (1992) *Working with the 'Unthinkable'*, London: Family Planning Association.

Brown, H., Stein, J., and Turk, V. (1995) 'Report of a second two-year incidence survey on the reported sexual abuse of adults with learning disabilities: 1991–1992,' *Mental Handicap Research* 8, 1.

Buchanan, A. and Oliver, J.E. (1977) 'Abuse and neglect as a cause of mental retardation', *British Journal of Psychiatry,* 131, pp.458–467.

Bull, R. (1994) 'Interviewing people with communicative disabilities', in Bull, R. and Carson, D. (eds.) (1994) *Handbook of Psychology in Legal Contexts*, Chichester: J.Wiley.

Channel 4 (1993) *Breaking the Silence: An Edited Transcript,* London: Channel 4.

Carson, D. (1990) *Professionals and the Courts: A Handbook for Expert Witnesses*, Birmingham: Venture Press.

Clare, I. (unpublished) Training notes, Department of Developmental Psychiatry, Cambridge.

Cohen, S. and Warren, R. (1987) 'Preliminary survey of family abuse of children served by United Cerebral Palsy Centre', *Developmental Medicine and Child Neurology,* 29, pp.12–18.

CPS (1994) *The Code for Crown Prosecutors*, London: Crown Prosecution Service.

Craft, A. (ed.) (1992) 'Sexuality, special issue', *Mental Handicap*, 20,2 .

CSDHA (1992) 'Violence against women' (special issue), *Women 2000*, no.4. Vienna: Centre for the advancement of women, Vienna International Centre.

Department of Health and Welsh Office (1993) *Code of Practice - Mental Health Act 1983*. London: HMSO

Dunne, T.P. and Power, A. (1990) 'Sexual abuse and mental handicap: preliminary findings of a community-based study', *Mental Handicap Research*, 3, 2, pp.111–125.

Dyer, C. (1992a.) 'US witness in London civil case to testify by video link', *The Guardian*, May 13, p.4.

Dyer, C. (1992b.) 'Court film may cheat death', *The Guardian*, June 25, p.1.

Dyer, C. (1992c.) 'Public bodies cannot sue to deflect critics', *The Guardian*, February 20, p.4.

Fattah E.A. (1989) *The Plight of Victims in Modern Society*. London: Macmillan.

Fattah, E. A. (1993) 'Doing unto others: the revolving roles of victim and victimizer', *Simon Frazer University Alumni Journal*, Winter.

Ferriman, A. (1992) 'Killing reveals no checks on private care of elderly', *Observer*, 19 Jan, p.5.

Fraser, G. (1993) 'Going to court', *NAPSAC Bulletin No.6*. Nottingham: National Association for the Protection from Sexual Abuse of Adults and Children with Learning Difficulties.

Furey, E. and Haber, M. (1989) 'Protecting adults with mental retardation: a model statute', *Mental Retardation* 27, 3, pp.135–140.

Greenwich Social Services (1993) *Recognising and Responding to the Abuse of Adults with Learning Disabilities*, Greenwich: Greenwich Social Services.

Guardian (1992) 'Teacher denies 23 charges of sex abuse at special school', *The Guardian*, February 13, p.2.

Gudjonsson, G., Clare, I., Rutter, S., Pearse, J. (1993) *Persons at Risk During Interviews in Police Custody: The Identification of Vulnerabilities, Royal Commission on Criminal Justice*, London:HMSO.

Gunn, M.J. (1986) 'Human Rights and people with mental handicaps', *Mental Handicap*, 14, September, pp.116–120.

Gunn, M.J. (1990) 'The law and learning disability', *International Review of Psychiatry*, 2, pp.13–22.

Halsbury's Laws of England (1993) 4th edition. London: Butterworths.

Hart, T. (1992) 'Make your own choices', *Disability Issues* 9, p.3.

Haseltine, B. and Miltenberger, R.G. (1990) 'Teaching self-protection skills to persons with mental retardation', *American Journal on Mental Retardation*, 95(2), pp.188–197.

Hayes, S. (1993) *People with an Intellectual Disability and the Criminal Justice System,* New South Wales: New South Wales Law Reform Commission.

Heptinstall, D. (1994) 'Sexual abuse: justice means too many hurdles', *Community Living*, April, pp.7–9.

Hewitt, S. (1987) 'The abuse of deinstitutionalised persons with mental handicaps', *Disability Handicap and Society*, 2 (2), pp.127–135.

Home Office (1990) *Victims' Charter*, London: Home Office. (For details please contact: Home Office Public Relations Branch, Queen Anne's Gate, London SW1H 9AT.)

Johnson, K., Andrew, R., Topp, V. (1988) *Silent Victims: A Study of People with Intellectual Disabilities as Victims of Crime*, Carlton (Australia): Office of the Public Advocate.

Jones, R. (1993) *Registered Homes Act Manual*, London: Sweet and Maxwell.

Jones, J. (1993) 'Mum told to lock up her Down's daughter', *The Observer*, 19 December, p.2.

JSB (1994) *Oaths and Oath-Taking*, London: Judicial Studies Board.

Köhnken, G. (1990) 'The evaluation of statement credibility: social judgement and expert diagnostic approaches', in Spencer, J., Nicholson, G., Flin, R., Bull, R. (eds) *Children's Evidence in Legal Proceedings: An International Perspective*, Cambridge: Faculty of Law.

Korn, Y. and McDougal, J. (1993) *Inspirations for Action: A Practical Guide to Women's Safety*, Swindon: Crime Concern.

Law Commission (1991) *Mentally Incapacitated Adults and Decision-Making: An Overview*, London: HMSO.

Liberty (1993) *People with Mental Health Problems and Learning Disability,* London: Liberty/MIND

Lord Chancellor's Department (1992) *Courts Charter*, London: HMSO. (New edition, *Charter for Court Users* due for publication July 1995. For details please contact: Court Service, Customer Service and Communications Branch, Southside, 105 Victoria Street, London SW1E 6QT. Tel: 0171-210 1676/1689.)

Magistrates' Association (1993) *Sentencing Guidelines*, London: Magistrates' Association.

Mansell, J. L. (1993) *Services for People with Learning Disabilities and Challenging Behaviour or Mental Health Needs*, HMSO: London.

Marchant, R. and Page, M. (1992) *Bridging the Gap*, London: NSPCC.

Morgan, J. and Zedner, L. (1992) *Child Victims*, Oxford: Clarendon Press.

NAPSAC (1993) *It Could Never Happen Here*, Chesterfield: ARC/NAPSAC.

NDT (1993) Response of the National Development team and the Norah Fry Research Centre to the Law Commission Consultation Paper No.129, (unpublished) Manchester: NDT.

NSPCC (1993) *The Child Witness Pack*, NSPCC/Childline: London.

Nursing Times (1992) 'Suffering acts of omission', *Nursing Times*, June 17, 6, 39, pp.50–51.

Pritchard, J. (1992) *Guide to the Law*, Viking: Harmondsworth.

Renton, A. (1993) 'Woman sues over school bullying', *The Independent,* p.3.

Ridout, S. (1993) *Abuse and Adults with Learning Difficulties: Reducting the Risk*, Warwick: University of Warwick, Department of Applied Social Studies.

Roeher (1988) *Vulnerable: Sexual Abuse and People with an Intellectual Handicap*, Ontario: The G Allen Roeher Institute.

Roeher (1992) *No More Victims: A Manual to Guide the Police in Addressing the Sexual Abuse of People With Mental Handicap*, Ontario: The G Allen Roeher Institute.

Schroeder, I. (1991) 'Screen tests', *Social Work Today*, 5 December, pp.15–17.

Senn, C. (1988) *Vulnerable: Sexual Abuse and People With an Intellectual Handicap*. Ontario: Roeher Institute.

Simons, K. (1992) *Sticking Up for Yourself: Self-Advocacy of People with Learning Disabilities*, Joseph Rowntree Foundation: York.

Sinason, V. (1992) *Mental Handicap and the Human Condition: New Approaches from the Tavistock*, Free Association Books: London

Singhal, S. (1992) 'Under suspicion for a crime they don't understand', *The Independent*, 4 September.

Sherrat, T. (1992) 'Incompetent council let children suffer', *The Guardian*, November 24, p.5.

Sobsey, D. (1994) *'Violence and Abuse in the Lives of People with Disabilities – The End of Silent Acceptance?* Baltimore: Paul H. Brookes Publishing Co.

Sone, K. (1993) 'Challenging behaviour', *Community Care* 14 October, issue 988, p.20.

Taylor, P. (1993) 'A study to evaluate course teaching self-protection skills against sexual abuse to young women with a moderate learning disability, with a view to improving future teaching methods', unpublished MSc Dissertation, Department of Psychology, University of Portsmouth.

Tharinger, D., Horton, C.B., Millea, S. (1990) 'Sexual abuse and exploitation of children and adults with mental retardation and other handicaps', *Child abuse and neglect*, 14, pp.301–312.

Thompson, D., Whitney, I., Smith, P. K. (1994) 'Bullying of children with special needs in mainstream schools', *Support for Learning*, 9,3, pp.103–106.

Wade, A. (1993) 'The Canadian experience', *Community Care*, 4 February, pp.24–25.

Ward, D. (1994) 'Disabled woman sues over "bullies"', *The Guardian*, June 7, p.2.

Westcott, H. L. (1993) *Abuse of Children and Adults with Disabilities*, London: NSPCC.

Whoriskey, M., Green A. M., McKay, C. (1993) *Consenting Adults? Sexual Abuse and Adults with Learning Disabilities – A Framework for Practice Guidelines*, ENABLE: Glasgow.

Williams, C. (1993a.) *The Right to be Known,* Bristol: Norah Fry Research Centre.

Williams, C. (1993b.) 'Vulnerable victims? a current awareness of the victimisation of people with learning difficulties', *Disability, Handicap and Society*, 8, 2, pp.161–172.

Williams, C. (1993c) Who are 'Street Children?' A hierarchy of street use and appropriate responses. *Child abuse and neglect*, 17, pp.831–841.

Williams, C. (1995) *Cracking Crime – A Learning Pack* (including video), Brighton: Pavilion Publishing.

WWG (1994) *Walsall Women's Group Safety Video – No Means No,* from: The women's Group, The College of Continuing Education in Walsall, Whitehall School, Weston Street, Walsall WS1 4BQ.

Index